**THE BOO̶**
**THE WORLD LAUGH WITH YOU**

You get a wonderful double dose of laughter in this joke jamboree.

First your own laughter when you read the more than one thousand riddles, quips, one-liners, and funny, funny stories on every subject from sports to sex, bathrooms to boardrooms, clergymen to swingers, and nuts to shrinks.

Then the laughter when you tell the jokes you choose to the people you aim to delight.

So if you like your humor with an up-to-date twist and a surefire tickle, this is the collection that begins where all the others leave off.

# 1001 *MORE* GREAT JOKES

JEFF ROVIN, a writer for *MAD* magazine, is the author of *1001 Great Jokes, TV Babylon, In Search of Trivia,* and *The Second Signet Book of Movie Lists* (all available in Signet editions).

# 1,001 MORE GREAT JOKES

## JEFF ROVIN

A SIGNET BOOK

SIGNET
Published by New American Library, a division of
Penguin Putnam Inc., 375 Hudson Street,
New York, New York 10014, U.S.A.
Penguin Books Ltd, 27 Wrights Lane,
London W8 5TZ, England
Penguin Books Australia Ltd, Ringwood,
Victoria, Australia
Penguin Books Canada Ltd, 10 Alcorn Avenue,
Toronto, Ontario, Canada M4V 3B2
Penguin Books (N.Z.) Ltd, 182–190 Wairau Road,
Auckland 10, New Zealand

Penguin Books Ltd, Registered Offices:
Harmondsworth, Middlesex, England

First published by Signet, an imprint of New American Library,
a division of Penguin Putnam Inc.

First Printing, May 1989
17  16  15  14  13  12

# INTRODUCTION

With all the great literature on sale in our nation's bookstores, critics have openly wondered how *1,001 Great Jokes* managed to sell so many copies that it demanded a sequel. The answer is simple: people preferred it to the alleged classics. Here, for example, is an exchange which was actually overheard in a typical bookshop.

A woman walked over to the clerk and asked, "Have you ever read Poe?"

"No, ma'am," he replied. "I've always read rather well."

"You don't understand. I mean Edgar Allan Poe—Poe's *Raven*."

"Is he? And what's *he* got to be sore about?"

The woman frowned. "Forget it. Do you carry *Ben-Hur*?"

"Certainly not. Much too racy."

"*The Hobbit?*"

"We don't."

"You don't what?"

"We don't hobbit in stock."

"What about *Antigone*?"

"No . . . just the one about Uncle Tom."

"*Decameron?*"

"Yes, ma'am—in case we're robbed."

"*Harte?*"

"No. All you do is throw a switch."

"Sir, I mean I want *Bret*—"

"Sam's Bakery, around the corner."

"Christ, what are you an idiot?"

"No, ma'am. Just a myshkinthrope."

The woman looked around. "Hey, am I on *Candid Camera?* Is this one great joke?"

The clerk smiled. "Ah, you mean *1,001 Great Jokes!* Yes, ma'am, we have that book in stock."

The woman bought it, and the moral, of course, is that the first volume sold not because of highbrows and lowbrows, but because readers browse.

Unwilling to tamper with great literature (or success), we have assembled all the great jokes, riddles, and puns we weren't able to include in the first volume. Once again we arranged them by topic, dictionary-style, all of them extensively cross-referenced.

Many of the most popular categories in the first book are represented once again, such as Sex, Masturbation, Prostitutes, and Psychiatrists (good company you keep, Freud). There are also dozens of new categories, an eclectic bunch which ranges from Cartoon Characters to Chewing Gum to World War II, as well as topical subjects such as Nicaragua and the Deficit.

And, just to prove that we haven't acquired any

taste since the first book, we've also added entries on Sodomy, the Polish (along with the Irish, Italians, and Jews), and Jesus Christ, among many others.

The critics, of course, will still look down their noses at those of us who like a good laugh. However, take heart in the fact that no less a literary figure than Jane Austen is on *our* side. As her character, the witty Mr. Bennett, asks in *Pride and Prejudice*, "For what do we live, but to make sport for our neighbours, and laugh at them in our turn?"

## ABORTION

1. Q: What do they call an aborted fetus in Czechoslovakia?
   A: A canceled Czech.

2. Then there was the cow that, for the sake of her health, was given an abortion. Or, as the witty veterinarian put it, she was decaffeinated. . . .

## ABSENTMINDEDNESS

1. Professors are known to be absentminded, but nothing tops the teacher who undid his vest, held his necktie, and pissed in his pants.

2. Ms. Thomas, the vice-president of sales, was having lunch in the executive dining room with another v-p.

   "I swear," Ms. Thomas said, "my assistant is so absentminded it's a wonder he sells as many computers as he does. I asked him to bring me a newspaper on the way back from lunch—and I'll bet he forgets."

   Just then the assistant ran into the v-p's office. "Ms. Thomas, guess what!" he hooted. "While I was eating, Mr. Grayzel of Grayzel Publishing sat down next to me. Started talking about how he needs a new computer system. By the time we finished eating, he agreed to buy a quarter-million-dollar system from us!"

The v-p turns to her colleague. "What did I tell you? He forgot the newspaper."

## ACCENTS

1. While doing his homework, a little Jewish boy asks his father, "Dad, can you tell me what a vacuum is?"

   "Surely, son. A vaccum is a void."

   "I know," the boy replies, "but vat's dat void mean?"

2. Running up the road to church, Mrs. Carter saw a man headed in the opposite direction.

   "Tell me," she panted, "is mass out?"

   "Nope," the man replied, "but yer hat's on crooked."

3. After creating a new engine in 1911, the inventor had no idea what to call it. Until, that is, a little Jewish man boarded the train on which the engine was being used.

   Looking it over, and admiring the sleek, shiny wheels, the passenger remarked, "Hmmm. Dees'll sure go qvick."

4. "Did you hear?" Moshe said. "Old Nehemiah had his arm amputated."

"Really?" said Mordecai. "At vich joint?"

Moshe frowned. "That's some way to talk about the hospital, Mordecai."

5. Visiting the zoo on his first-ever trip to San Diego, a Scotsman paused by one of the cages.

"Lord," he said, "an' what animal is that, then?"

Overhearing him, the keeper said, "That, sir, is a moose."

"A moose!" he said. "Kee-rist! An' I suppose ye've got rats the size of elephants, then?"

6. "Dis is de happiest day of my life!" said Abe, patting his grandson on the back. The other men in the old age home looked over. "Today, my friends, dis brilliant grandson of mine, he graduated from medical school."

One of the men asked the graduate, "NYU?"

Abe shot him a look. "And vy not?"

7. Flipping through the mail, Mrs. Dorchester found a strange-sounding invitation.

"Look at this," she said to her husband. "It's from that Italian family which moved in next door. But—I can't figure out what it says."

Looking at it, Mr. Dorchester read aloud, "Gina Mr. U, 2 wedding." After studying it for a moment, he said, "I think you'd better buy a nice gift."

"Whatever for?"

"Because it says, 'Gina missed her period. You comma to wedding.' "

8. With time to kill before boarding the flight back to Japan, the tourist went to the currency exchange at Los Angeles International Airport.

After the agent had counted out the money, the tourist stared at it, aghast. "Say! When I arrive, I get twice as many dorrars for yen."

Looking down her nose at the Oriental gentleman, the clerk said, "Fluctuations."

Stiffening, the man said, "Well, fluck you Amelicans, too!"

**ACTORS**     *See also* MOTION PICTURES, CRITICS 3,
SPERM BANKS 4

1. Movie star Dirk Daring has a problem. He makes a fortune doing action movies, but he's a coward at heart, and refuses to do his own stunts. Reading of Dirk's problem in one of the tabloids, Dr. Brinkenstein approaches him with an offer: for a quarter of a million dollars, he'll clone Dirk. The duplicate can take all the risks, and Dirk can take all the credit.

The star agrees. However, on the night that Brinkenstein delivers the copy to Dirk's penthouse apartment, something goes wrong. The clone rips off all his clothes and goes running around the building. Dirk chases him, and finally corners the clone on the rooftop. Unfortunately, when Dirk goes to grab the clone, the bare doppelganger slips and falls twenty-eight stories to his death.

Minutes later, the police arrive. They take Dirk into custody, but he dismisses the charges of murder.

"I had that man manufactured," he said. "It isn't real. It's just a clone. There are no grounds for arrest."

Scratching his head, one of the officers says, "On the contrary, Mr. Daring, we have every reason to take you in."

"Oh yeah? For what?"

The officer replies, "For making an obscene clone fall."

2. In the midst of overacting the part of Hamlet, the diabetic actor suddenly fell to the floor, unconscious. Rushing to the stage, a doctor quickly shoved Junior Mints into his mouth, and in less than a minute the actor had recovered.

"That was amazing, doc!" said a stagehand. "How did you know what to do?"

"Elementary," the physician replied. "Haven't you ever heard of sugar-cured ham?"

3. Sylvester Spillane and Kevin Kaline were movie stars from the brawn and introspection school, respectively. While making a movie together, Sylvester crowed, "Y'know, my analyst is the toughest dude in the world. He could wreck *your* shrink with his little finger."

"Perhaps," Kevin said quietly, "but *my* psychiatrist could rid yours of his compulsive aggression."

4. Watching the movie star as he stepped from his limousine, one old woman turned to another.

   "To think," she said, "I read in *People* that his parents didn't even want him to become an actor."

   "I saw his last film," said the other. "They got their wish."

5. Q: How are an actor and a rabbi different?
   A: You might want to take a look at the actor's collection of clippings. . . .

6. Then there was the actor who reluctantly turned down a role in a Broadway play.

   "Why?" asked the startled director. "It's a great part!"

   "I know, but I have a TV series to do."

   "Hell, that doesn't start for five months."

   "I know," said the actor, "but it says right here in your script that the second act is one year later."

## ACUPUNCTURE

1. Needles may work for many people, but not for the moron who turned to acupuncture because he was suffering from hemophilia.

*See also* HEAVEN 2

1. After creating Adam and Eve, God took a look at them and realized that while they were different, they were not dissimilar enough. Thus he split the difference.

2. Q: According to the Bible, how were the Irish created?
   A: Adam looked down at Eve and said, "Oh! Hair!" And Eve looked down at Adam and said, "Oh! Tool!"

3. Q: After inventing the Irish, what else did Adam and Eve create?
   A: Computers. She had an apple, he had a wang.

4. Discovering that her mate was allergic to fig leaves, Eve prepared a lotion to spread on his sensitive areas. It was the world's first Adam balm. . . .

5. Q: If Eve wore a fig leaf, what did Adam wear?
   A: A hole in it.

6. A Texan, a Frenchman, and a Russian were discussing the Old Testament.
   "Adam and Eve had to be Texans," the Texan said. "I mean, only a gentleman from

Texas would share his only apple with a lady."

"You are mistaken," said the Frenchman. "They were French. How else could they have been so much in love?"

The Russian said, "You are both wrong! Who but a Russian would walk around with no clothes, have nothing but an apple to share between them, and think they were in paradise?"

7. While lounging beneath a willow one morning, Adam looked up and was surprised to see Eve, naked, streak by. Moments later, God called down and asked to speak to the woman.

"Sorry," Adam said sheepishly, "but Eve is absent without leaf!"

**ADVERTISING**    *See also* AUTOMOBILE ACCIDENTS 4

1. It was the latest thing in TV promotions: short, short commercials based on one punchy, action-packed word. The format was dubbed, naturally, "adverbs."

2. It was an ad which caught peoples' eye: the hotel manager wrote that she was looking for people who were inn-experienced.

1. While making his final approach to the airport, the captain of the 747 came on the loudspeaker.

   "In just a few minutes, we will be landing at Chicago's O'Hare Airport. I want to thank you for flying with us, and hope you choose to do so again."

   Unfortunately, the captain neglected to shut the loudspeaker off again. Thus the entire cabin heard him say to his copilot, "When we land, the first thing I'm gonna take me a piss and a crap. And the second thing I'm gonna do is give that redheaded stewardess a tumble she'll never forget."

   Mortified, the stewardess in question dashed madly toward the cockpit. Enroute, an elderly woman grabbed her elbow.

   "Slow down, honey," she said. "He's got something else to do first."

2. A pair of eagles were flying over the Rockies when a jet dashed by.

   "Christ," said one, "look at that sonofagun move!"

   "Well," said the other, "you'd move too if you had four assholes and they were all on fire."

3. During the transoceanic flight, the pilot of the jumbo jet suddenly notices that one of the

engines has shut down. As calmly as possible he says into the p.a. system, "Ladies and gentlemen, there's no need to be alarmed, but one of our engines has gone down and we'll be arriving about forty-five minutes late."

A few minutes later, a second engine fails. "Ladies and gentlemen," says the captain, "I regret to inform you that a second engine has shut down. We can still fly, but we'll have to take it slow, and will be two hours late."

Not a half hour passes and a third engine ceases to function. With just a bit of trepidation the pilot informs the passengers, "Ladies and gentlemen, we have just one engine left. It will keep us airborne, but I regret that we'll be four hours late."

Hearing the announcement, one moron says to her companion, "Christ! If that last engine goes out, we'll be up here all day!"

## AMNESIA

1. Steiner looked suspiciously at the waiter. "Say— haven't I seen you somewhere before?"

"I don't believe so," the waiter replied, and took Steiner's order.

When he returned with the appetizer, Steiner said, "Were you stationed in Casablanca in '42?"

"No, sir."

When he returned with the main course,

Steiner asked, "Did you ever work for the Belock Corporation?"

"Never, sir."

Steiner continued to ponder the problem, and when the man returned with his dessert, the customer's face brightened. "I know!" he said suddenly. "Aren't you the guy who took my order?"

2. "Doc!" the man screamed, "I've lost my memory!"

"Calm down, man. When did this happen."

The man looked at him. "When did what happen?"

## ANIMALS

*See also* BIRDS, CATS, COWS, DOGS, ELEPHANTS, GOATS, HORSES, INSECTS, LIONS, NOAH'S ARK, PIGS, RABBITS, SEALS, SKUNKS

1. Deep in the woods, a trio of animals were discussing who among them was the most powerful.

"I am," said the hawk, "because I can fly and swoop down swiftly at my prey."

"I am," said the mountain lion, "because I am not only fleet, but I have powerful teeth and claws."

"I am," said the skunk, "because with a flick of my tail, I can drive off the two of you."

Suddenly a huge grizzly lumbered over and settled the debate by eating them all, hawk, lion, and stinker.

# ANTIQUES

*See also* SEX 13

1. As one antique dealer admitted to another, theirs was a strange way of making a living. "In what other business," she asked, "do grandparents buy something, parents sell it, and children buy it again?"


# APARTMENTS

1. It's a sad day when inflation is such that it's no longer the tenants who are breaking leases, but vice versa. . . .


# ARABS

*See also* HOMOSEXUALS 7, LAVATORIES 2

1. Q: Why is the camel called the ship of the desert?
   A:  Because it's filled with arab semen.

2. While walking down the street in Belfast, Isaac Goldstein felt a knife pressed to his back.
   "Catholic or Protestant," a voice demanded.
   "Jewish," Goldstein replied.
   "Well, then," said the voice, "I am surely the luckiest Arab in all of Ireland!"

1. After a famous eye doctor saved his fading sight, the renowned artist painted a tribute to the surgeon: a huge op-art picture of an eye in the lobby of the doctor's building. The giant orb was red and brown, with long, tendril-like lashes, a lush blue brow, an iris painted in Day-Glo green, and, in the midst of the painting, a portrait of the doctor herself.

   Passing the work one day, the honoree asked a fellow doctor, "So, what do you think?"

   "I have just one thing to say," he responded. "Thank the good Lord you aren't a gynecologist."

2. Taking up painting, asylum inmate Van Goon worked for weeks on his masterpiece. When he finally showed it to asylum doctors, they were stunned. The canvas was entirely blank.

   "It's lovely," said one psychiatrist, "but, er . . . what is it?"

   "Why," he proudly replied, "It is a painting of the exodus from Egypt."

   "I see," said another doctor. "Actually, what I *don't* is the Red Sea."

   "Ah," said the inmate, "it's been parted . . . driven back, as it says in the Old Testament."

   "And the Israelites?"

   "They have already passed through."

   "And what of the Egyptians?" demanded another.

"Christ, are you blind?" said the artist, growing indignant. "They haven't arrived yet!"

3. Under protest, the photographer accompanies his girlfriend to the opening of a one-man show, a selection of one artist's abstracts. Encountering the painter at the gallery, the photographer says, "Y'know, you people really piss me off. Look at this. All this work is just dribbling on canvas, splashes of paint that don't mean a goddam thing." He read the card beneath one painting. "A portrait of your love, huh? What happened to her? Did she get caught in a blender? Christ, man, I like realistic work. I like to look at a friggin' picture and see it exactly the way it is."

Calmly the artist said, "I see you're a man of strong opinions. Tell me, have you taken any good photographs lately?"

"As a matter of fact, I have," the photographer said, and reached into his wallet. "It's a study of my mother, Jean."

After examining the snapshot the artist said, "Incredible. Is she really this small?"

## ASTRONOMY

1. Called to the scene of a spectacular celestial display, the astronomer watched as a bright object dashed through the skies over Vaghi, New Mexico.

When he returned to his observatory, reporters asked him if what he'd seen was really a UFO.

Looking them straight in the eye, the stoic scientist replied, "No comet."


**AUTHORS**  *See also* CRITICS, LIONS 3, PRISON 1

1. Called on as an expert witness in a libel case, an author was asked to identify himself.

   "Irving Johns," he said in a stentorian voice, "the greatest American writer since Melville."

   During recess, his wife came over to him. "Honey—your testimony was wonderful, but don't you think you could have been a bit more modest when giving your name?"

   "My dear," the writer said, "I had no choice. I was under oath."


2. Then there was the author who suffered from writer's cramp—also known as authoritis.


3. "It is only right," wrote the critic, "that Mr. Crows is a highly paid novelist. After all, he has to read that stuff more than once."


4. After gaining fame with his moralistic tales, Aesop was vacationing at a Greek resort when he was recognized by a group of children.

   "Tell us a story, tell us a story!" cried one child.

Said another, "I want to hear the one about Jack and Jill."

Smiling paternally, Aesop patted the child on the head and said, "Sorry, but that's not my fable."

## AUTOMATION

See also INVENTORS, PROGRESS

1. Fascinated by the automatic milking machine, the pubescent young boy decided to place his member in one of the slots and have it milk him. The experiment proved highly successful, but when he was finished, he was unable to liberate himself. Reluctantly he called for his father.

   After examining the situation, the farmer headed for his truck.

   "Where are you going?" the boy cried.

   "To town, t'get oysters. That machine there is set at two quarts."

2. It was the first time Al had ever flown the SST, and he was amazed to find that it had a separate men's and women's room. Finding the men's room occupied, he slipped into the women's room. While sitting on the toilet, he noticed a series of buttons on the wall. Curious, he pushed one marked "WW." At once a stream of warm water jetted along the insides of his thighs. Delighted, he pushed the button marked "PP" beside it. The water shut down

and, oh so gently, a small powder puff began tapping his behind. Thrilled, he pushed the button labeled "ATR."

That was the last thing he remembered until he opened his eyes and looked up into the smiling face of the stewardess.

"Christ," he moaned, "what happened?"

"You went in the ladies' room," the woman scolded. "That's a no-no."

"Sorry . . . but I had to go!"

"And you pressed the 'ATR' button, didn't you?"

"Y-yes."

She smiled. "That stands for Automatic Tampon Removal. When you can walk, sir, you'll find your penis waiting for you in the seat pocket."


## AUTOMOBILE ACCIDENTS     *See also* AUTOMOBILES

1. A man had been crossing a street when a car slammed into him. The pedestrian sued the motorist, whose lawyer made the following statement at the end of the trial.

   "Your honor, my client was not at fault. He has been driving a car for thirty years, and has never had an accident, nor gotten so much as a speeding ticket. I do not think I need to say any more."

   Unimpressed, the lawyer for the plaintiff rose. "Your honor, since counsel insists on bringing up the matter of experience, may I remind the court that my client has been walking for over seventy years. . . ."

2. While driving along the highway, a motorist was surprised to see a police officer motioning for him to pull off the road. The man drove onto the shoulder and rolled down his window.

"What's the matter, officer? Was I going too fast?"

"No, bub—it's your wife! She fell out of the car two exits back!"

The man sighed. "Thank God! I thought I'd gone deaf!"

3. Moments after a terrible car accident, Josiah ran up to a man whose left hand had been severed.

"Relax, fella," he said reassuringly, "you'll be all right in no time."

4. Then there was the body shop which advertised to automobile owners by asking, "May we have the next dents?"

**AUTOMOBILES**   *See also* AUTOMOBILE ACCIDENTS, DRUNKS 2, INFIDELITY 4, TEENAGERS 3, WEALTH 1, WORDPLAY 3

1. Unable to find a replacement cog for his car engine, a Datsun owner is told he'll have to go pick one up at the factory in Japan. Rather

than fly over and get just one, he decides to pick up four dozen cogs.

As fate would have it, on the way home, just shy of the airport the airplane begins leaking fuel. In order to conserve as much gasoline as possible, the pilot orders that all baggage be jettisoned. Reluctantly the man allows his replacement parts to be thrown overboard.

Below, a couple looks up from their porch.

"Look, Miriam!" the man declares. "It's raining Datsun cogs!"

2. Then there was the automobile manufacturer who decided to name his new female-skewed model after Queen Elizabeth instead of Joan of Arc. After all, Joan was only a wonder, while Elizabeth was a Tudor.

3. Lastly, when it comes to automobiles, it's tough to drive a bargain.

## BACHELORS                    *See also* DATING

1. Though he admitted to adoring women, the bachelor insisted he would never marry. Said he: "I can be miss-led only so far."

1. Hoping to improve his business on the Fourth of July, the baker introduced an inspired new cake frosting: Of Thee Icing.

## BALDNESS

1. "George," said the woman, "my hair is falling out. What can I use to keep it in?"
   The hairdresser replied, "Might I suggest a shoebox?"

2. As the saying goes, it's better to be bald on the outside than on the inside. . . .

## BANKING          *See also* BANKRUPTCY, THE IRS, LIFESTYLE

1. Interviewing the young Swede for a job as teller, the bank president is amazed with the skill the applicant exhibits at handling money.
   "So," the president says, "where did you get your training?"
   "Yale," the fair-haired youth replies.
   "I see. And what did you say your name was?"
   He answers, "Yackson."

2. Strolling into a bank, the moron presented a check and asked the teller to cash it. The

teller informed the woman that she must first identify herself.

Pulling a mirror from a purse, the woman looked into it and said, "Yes, sir—it's me, all right."

3. Sick and tired of having to balance his wife Harriet's checkbook, Howie made a deal with her: he would only look at it after *she* had spent a few hours trying to wrestle it into shape. Only then would he lend his expertise.

The following night, after spending hours poring over stubs and figures, the woman said proudly, "There! I've done it! I made it balance!"

Impressed, Howie came over to take a look. "Let's see . . . mortgage $615.42 . . . electricity $90.20 . . . phone $45.45." His brow furrowed as he read the last entry. "It says here ESP, $310.70. What the heck is that?"

"Oh," she said, "that means, Error Some Place."

**BANKRUPTCY**  *See also* BANKING, THE STOCK MARKET

1. More often than not, bankruptcy is due to both a lack and a lass.

2. And, of course, you can try paying your debts with a smile, but the bank will still want money.

1. As they were crossing the players' parking lot, a pair of New York ball players noticed a baseball groupie giving a minor leaguer a hand job in his car.

   "Well, how about that?" one of the players said. "It took a yanker to finally make him a yankee."

2. When she was finished with the bush leaguer, the groupie got on the team bus and everyone got off.

3. Q: Why does Don Mattingly make so much money each year?
   A: A good batter always makes good dough.

4. Q: Why is baseball like wooing a JAP?
   A: You can't begin to do either without a diamond.

5. Then there was the baseball superstar who had no trouble getting to first base with his female admirers. Unfortunately, he was thrown out at home.

1. After he was arrested for bigamy, the guilty man was heard to remark, homophonically, "It's the first time I ever heard of two rites making a wrong!"

2. Then there was the bigamist who loved not wisely but two well.


## BIOLOGY

1. Conducting research on grasshoppers, the Polish entomologist rang a buzzer next to the insect's cage. The insect began leaping about, and the scientist recorded the reaction in his notebook.

    Next, he amputated one of the insect's legs, and once again sounded the buzzer. The grasshopper jumped again, albeit with much less success.

    Then he removed all of the grasshopper's legs and returned it to the cage. This time when he rang the buzzer, it just lay there.

    The researcher wrote, "It is proven, therefore, that when a grasshopper's legs are severed, the insect goes deaf."

1. Q: What's the difference between a canary
   with one wing and one with two wings?
   A: A difference of a pinion.

2. When a rundown section of town was condemned, the goods from its various buildings
   were sold. This included a parrot, who ended
   up in an exclusive pet store and was sold to an
   older woman.

   Despite every effort the woman was unable
   to get the parrot to talk. She coaxed it, offered
   it crackers, but the bird wouldn't say a word.

   One night the woman's bridge club was
   playing at her home, and the conversation
   turned to the comfort of their respective panty
   hose. Deciding to check the labels, they hitched
   up their dresses.

   "Finally," the bird squawked, "home sweet
   home. Now will one of you whores gimme a
   smoke?"

3. Q: What do you get when you cross a disobedient dog with a rooster?
   A: A cock that doesn't come.

4. Q: What's the difference between an awful
   marksperson and a constipated owl?
   A: One shoots and never hits. . . .

5. Q: What's the difference between a gull and a diaperless infant?
   A: One flits on the shore. . . .

6. While migrating south, one crow turned to another and to relieve the tedium struck up a conversation.
   "So," it said, "have you bred any good rooks lately?"

## BIRTH CONTROL
*See also* CONDOMS, PREGNANCY, IRANIANS 5

1. Q: What's a diaphragm?
   A: A trampoline for dickheads.

2. Q: What's a birth control pill?
   A: The other thing a woman can put in her mouth to keep from becoming pregnant.

3. Q: What is a diaphragm?
   A: A sock in the puss.

## BLACKS
*See also* DATING 4, GOD 2, LANGUAGES 7, LITERATURE 7, NICARAGUA 7, ORGASMS 1, PREGNANCY 1, PREJUDICE 9, 11, PROPOSALS 2, RESTAURANTS 15

1. Q: Why are there so few black nuns?
   A: Because they have trouble saying "superior" after "mother."

2. Mrs. Dupre stood before her first graders. "Now then, children: if anyone can spell 'before' and use it in a sentence, they will not have to take this morning's spelling test."

Hands shot up, and the teacher called on little Lisa.

"B-E-E-F . . ."

"No," the teacher said, "that isn't correct."

She called on little Tony, who said, "B-E-F-O-U-R . . ."

"No, Anthony, that isn't correct either."

She called on little Leroy, who rose and said confidently, "B-E-F-O-R-E."

"Very good!" the teacher exclaimed. "Now, can you use it in a sentence?"

Leroy's brow knit in thought. Then he said, "I'm gonna hit dis golf ball, so I guess dis be fore!"

3. Q: What is "xx"?
A: A black cosigning for a Pole.

**THE BLIND** *See also* THE HANDICAPPED, GYNECOLOGISTS 2, PROSTITUTES 2

1. Browsing through the department store with a friend, the blind woman picked up a cheese grater and quickly returned it to the shelf. Making a face, she said, "Such violent books they're writing these days!"

## BRASSIERES

See also CLOTHING

1. Q: What's the best way to catch a living bra?
   A: With a booby trap.

2. Q: What did the brassiere say to the hat?
   A: "You go on ahead, pal. I'm gonna give these two a lift."

## BULLS

See also COWS, POLITICIANS 5

1. Q: What's the best way to make a bull sweat?
   A: Give him a tight jersey.

## BUSINESS

See also ANTIQUES 1,
LUMBER 1, PANHANDLERS 2, 4

1. After just six months on the job, the board of directors of a major corporation voted to remove the CEO, who had cost the company millions of dollars. So vitriolic was the dismissal, in fact, that the press release was unusually candid: "Mr. Thomas has been relieved of his duties," it read simply, "for doing to our company exactly what panty hose did for finger fucking."

1. "Lucifer," said the teacher, "do you think you could explain to the class the difference between 'like' and 'love'?"

   "Well," said the boy, "I like my parents . . . but I love Milk Duds."

2. Little Sally came running in from school. "Mommy! Mommy! At show and tell, Billy showed us something that's six inches long, has two nuts, and can make me very fat!"

   Gasping, the woman said, "Sally! What on earth did he show you?"

   The girl replied, "An Almond Joy!"


## CANNIBALS

1. After the feast the cannibal approaches the chief's table and asks if he should clear away the plates.

   The chief looks around. "Yes," he says, "everyone's eaten."

2. Then there were the cannibals who captured a safari consisting entirely of politicians. They had to buy a crock pot to cook them.

3. Even more inconvenienced was the cannibal who was late coming home for dinner. His wife gave him the cold shoulder.

4. Entering the cannibal village, the missionary took the precaution of informing the chief that he was a strict vegetarian.

"That okay," said the chief, looking the newcomer over. "We here all strict humanitarians."

5. When the Soviet Union finally recognized the African nation of D'Bai, the D'Baian president paid a visit to Moscow. The Soviet foreign minister didn't like the proud, pro-Western official, and as he showed him around, he invited the D'Baian to particpate in a game of Russian roulette.

"What is that?" the president asked.

The Russian took him into a room, where there was a pistol lying on the table. He explained the rules, and manfully the president agreed to play.

The African placed the pistol to his head and pulled the trigger; the hammer clicked on an empty chamber.

A month later, it was the foreign minister's turn to visit D'Bai. There the president invited the Soviet to play a game of D'Baian roulette.

Remembering what he'd done to the D'Baian, the Russian was extremely anxious until he was shown to a room where six beautiful black women were perched naked on their knees.

The president said, "What you must do, my friend, is take your member and choose which of these women is to give you a blow job."

The Russian smiled. "I see. But—why is this called roulette? Where is the danger?"

The D'Baian replied, "One of the women is a cannibal."


**CARDS** *See also* GAMES, DOGS 5, HOMOSEXUALS 3,
LEPERS 2, MASTURBATION 1


1. Dr. Mason was watching television with his wife when the phone rang.

   "Mason, it's Dr. Briggs," said the voice on the other end. "We need a fourth for bridge. Think you can make it?"

   "Be right there," Mason replied.

   "What is it?" his wife asked.

   "Emergency," he said as he grabbed his medical kit and coat. "There are three doctors there already."


2. While giving a physical, the doctor noticed that his patient's shins were covered with dark, savage bruises.

   "Tell me," said the doctor, "do you play hockey or soccer?"

   "Neither," said the man. "My wife and I play bridge."

## CARTOON CHARACTERS

1. The judge looked down at Mickey Mouse, who was filing for divorce from Minnie Mouse.

   "Mr. Mouse," said the judge, "I'm afraid I can't grant your request for divorce. I've read the psychiatrist's report, and you simply have no grounds. Your wife is quite sane."

   "Sane?" squeaked Mickey. "I never said she was mad. What I said was that she's fucking Goofy!"

2. Splitting up with Daisy, Donald Duck visited a hooker and told her to put it on his bill. . . .

3. Q: After Mickey Mouse fell in the river, how did Mighty Mouse revive him?
   A: With mouse-to-mouse resuscitation.

## CASTAWAYS

1. Years ago, the six-year-old boy was sailing with his parents in the South Pacific when their boat sank. Only the boy made it to shore, staggering onto the golden sands of an uninhabited island.

   Years later, a young woman researching the islands for her Ph.D. in anthropology found the island and its inhabitant—who was now a young man with a bronze, impressive physique.

"Good lord," she said, "how long have you lived alone here?"

"As near as I can figure," he replied, "thirteen years."

"And how have you survived?"

"Actually, it hasn't been difficult at all. I pick berries, eat fruit, and dig for clams."

"What about sex?" she asked.

The young man said that he had no idea what sex was, and, rather than explain it, she removed her clothing and seduced the strapping youth right there on the beach.

When they were finished, she asked, "How did you like it?"

"Marvelous," he said, "but Christ—look what you did to my clam digger!"

2. "There I was," the grandfather said to his grandson, "shipwrecked in the middle of the Atlantic, with nothing to live on for two weeks but a can of tuna."

"Gee," said the boy, "it's a darn good thing it didn't tip over."

## CASTRO

*See also* MUSSOLINI, NICARAGUA, RUSSIA, STALIN

1. Going into a church in Havana, a poor woman paused by a cross and kissed the feet of Jesus.

"Tell me," asked a soldier, "would you

kiss the feet of your great leader Castro as well?"

The woman replied, "Why, yes—as long as he was hung this way."

2. Two Cubans were strolling through Havana on a pleasant summer day.

"What a lovely afternoon," one said. "I thank God for it."

"God?" the other sneered. "You should thank Castro."

"Castro? It was God who made those flowers smell so sweet."

"I would prefer to thank Castro."

"You're mad! It was God who made the water in the lake so clear and serene."

"I would prefer to thank Castro."

Stunned, the man said, "And who will you thank when Castro is dead?"

Replied the other: "God."

**CATS**                    See also DOGS, DRUNKS 6, LOGIC 1,
                            POLITICIANS 4, SENIOR CITIZENS 1

1. "Doctor," said the patient, "I need help! I can't stop acting like a cat!"

"How long have you had this problem?" the doctor asked.

"Let's see," said the patient, "Mom had the litter in '51. . . ."

2. Q: What did the man do after his cat was run over by a steamroller?
   A: He just sat there with a long puss.

3. Fascinated by her new pet kitten, little Jamie played with it day and night. The cat soon became exhausted, and curled up beside the fireplace to sleep. Comforted by the warmth, the animal began to purr.

   Screaming, Jamie ran into the bedroom. "Mommy, Mommy, come quickly! The kitty's beginning to boil!"

4. Then there was the cat who won the milk-drinking competition by seven laps.

5. Then there was the old woman who simply couldn't stop taking in stray cats. Finally, her landlady was forced to evict her. As she explained it to the woman, "We can no longer tolerate your add-a-puss complex."


**CELEBRITIES**          *See also* COUNTRY SINGERS 1,
     EGOTISTS 1, POLITICIANS 7, SEALS 3, TATOOS 1

1. Q: What do you get when you cross Billie Jean King with Bo Derek?
   A: A DC 10.

2. Q: What do you get when you cross the editor of *Cosmopolitan* with one of the Three Stooges?
   A: A Helen Curly Brown.

3. Q: What do you call Sophia Loren?
   A: A pizza ass.

4. As it happened, Errol Flynn and the aged priest died on the same day. However, the silver-tongued Flynn was able to finagle his way through the pearly gates before the clergyman arrived.

   Finally being admitted to heaven, the cardinal bumped into the late movie star.

   "Excuse me," he said, "but I want nothing more than to kneel and kiss the feet of the Virgin Mary. Do you know where I can find her?"

   Flynn grinned and said, "You're too late, Father."


**CEMETERIES**   *See also* LAWYERS 3, REINCARNATION 1

1. After a long night of drinking, friends Dube, Fats, and JW took a shortcut through a cemetery. Fats, who had imbibed more than his share, passed out cold near an open grave. His friends did not look forward to the prospect of carrying the big man home.

   "Hey," said Dube, "I have an idea. Why don't we put Fats in the grave? When he wakes up in the morning, he'll be so scared he'll think twice before ever getting drunk again."

   Finding an old coffin, the men closed it and

lowered Fats into the grave, then hid behind a tombstone to wait until morning.

Before long, the first rays of dawn broke over the cemetery and spilled into the open grave. All of a sudden the lid of the coffin flew into the sky, and an ebullient Fats sat up.

"Christ be praised!" he roared. "It's Judgment Day, and I'm the first one up!"

## CENSUS

1. Q: How is the census taken in Israel?
   A: They roll a quarter down the street.

2. Driving out to the boondocks of Arkansas, the census taker pulled up in front of a small farm. He approached a man who was rocking on the porch.

   "What're ya sellin', sonny?"

   "I'm not selling anything," the young man smiled. "I'm here to take the census."

   "The what?"

   "We're trying to find out just how many people live in the U.S."

   The farmer replied, "Then I'm afraid you wasted your time comin' out here. I haven't the faintest idea."

3. Knocking on the door of the small apartment, the census taker was greeted by a young woman.

   "Good morning," said the caller, "I'm taking the census and I'd like to ask you a few questions. Occupation?"

"Homemaker," replied the woman.

"Husband's occupation?"

"Manufacturer."

"Children?"

"No," said the woman. "Dresses."

## CHEFS
See also FOOD, RESTAURANTS

1. Realizing that more and more people are eating fine foods at home, a chef decided to open a phone line to counsel people on menus, recipes, and other food-related items.

   He began the service on the day before Thanksgiving, and it was extremely successful. Countless callers had to be put on hold while he answered questions, though no one seemed to mind the wait. However, on the second day, he received his first complaint.

   "You spoiled my turkey!" a woman yelled.

   "How so?" asked the chef.

   "When I called yesterday and asked you how long to cook it, you told me, 'Just a minute, madam.'"

2. The old Irish cook was famous for his bean soup. Stopping in at his Boston eatery, a tourist orders a bowl and is delighted.

   "I understand you use only 239 beans for this soup," says the tourist. "Why is that?"

" 'Tis obvious," the cook says. "If there were one more, it'd be too farty!"

3. Then there was the chef whose penis ached the entire time he studied at the Sorbonne. . . .

## CHESS

1. During a chess convention at a local hotel, the manager became extremely annoyed when the conventioneers stood around the lobby, discussing the game and blocking the way. Finally ordering them to their rooms, he said, "If there's one thing which makes me furious, it's chess nuts boasting by an open foyer!"

## CHEWING GUM

1. It was her first day on the job at the Double-Bubble plant, and Griselda fell into a vat of gum. Naturally, her boss chewed her out. . . .

## CHILDBIRTH

See also KIDS, DENTISTS 2, INSANE ASYLUMS 2, JAPANESE 1, 2, JEWISH AMERICAN PRINCESS 9

1. After his baby was born, the panicked Japanese father went to see the obstetrician.
   "Doctor," he said, "I don't mind telling you,

but I'm a little upset because my daughter has red hair. She can't possibly be mine."

"Nonsense," the doctor said. "Even though you and your wife both have black hair, one of your ancestors may have contributed red hair to the gene pool."

"It isn't possible," the man insisted. "We're pure Oriental."

"Well," said the doctor, "let me ask you this. How often do you have sex?"

The man seemed ashamed. "I've been working very hard for the past year. We only made love once or twice a month."

"There you have it!" the doctor said confidently. "It's just rust."

2. As it happened, three women in the Indian tribe were going to give birth at the same time. To make it as comfortable as possible, the chief ordered his braves to go out and fetch whatever kind of fur the women wanted to lie on.

The first woman asked for bearskin, the second for elk, the third for hippopotamus. Though it wasn't easy to find the latter, the braves returned with the hides in question.

In time, the first squaw had a son, who was six pounds, the second had a baby boy, who also weighed six pounds, and the third had a lad who tipped the scales at a remarkable thirteen pounds.

When informed of the births, the chief har-

rumphed and remarked, "It just goes to show—
the son of the squaw of the hippopotamus is
equal to the sons of the squaws of the other
two hides."

3. Lastly, as all parents discover, a baby is someone who must have a bottle or bust.

## CHRISTMAS  *See also* SANTA CLAUS

1. Returning to his apartment some weeks before Christmas, Anthony noticed an envelope
taped to his door. Opening it, he read, "From
your super—Merry Christmas."

Thinking that that was a nice gesture, he
put it from his mind. A week later, he found
another envelope taped to his door. This one
read, "From your super—Merry Christmas.
Second notice."

## THE CIRCUS  *See also* ENGAGEMENTS 3

1. Assigned to interview the midget of the circus
which has just rolled into town, Louanne went
to his trailer. A man well over six feet tall
answered the door.

"Excuse me," the reporter said, "but I'm
looking for Mr. Little."

"That's me," he said. Noticing her surprise,
he added, "This is my day off."

2. Then there was the circus strongman who was not only mighty, he was so strong that he carried the show.

3. He was certainly more of an asset than the circus accountant, who was fired when she was caught juggling the books.

4. After reading the morning newspaper, the Polish circus impresario bolted out the door and headed for the nearby military base.

   "Listen," he said to the sentry, "my side-show midget just died and I need to see Private Hargrove."

   "He's in the brig," said the sentry. "Besides, he's six-foot-two."

   "Really?" said the Pole. "Then that must've been a helluva big watch he slept on."

**CLERGY**   *See also* CONFESSION, EVANGELISTS, ACTORS 5, BLACKS 1, THE IRS 3, JESUS CHRIST, LIONS 1, MARRIAGE 5, POLICE 1, SEX 18

1. The order was such that the nuns were only permitted to say one word every year.

   At the end of the first year she was there, the novice was asked by the mother superior, "Tell me, sister. How do you like the food here?"

   "Stale," the novice replied.

   At the close of the following year, the mother

superior asked the sister, "How do you like your bed?"

"Hard," the sister answered.

At the conclusion of the third year, the mother superior asked the sister, "Will you be continuing here for a fourth year?"

"No," the woman said.

Indignant, the mother superior replied, "Well, I'm not surprised! You've been here for three years now, and all you've done is bitch, bitch, bitch!"

2. Walking into a liquor store, Sister Isabel asked the clerk for a bottle of vodka.

"My word," said the young man, "I could never live with myself if I sold alcohol to a sister!"

"It's all right," Isabel assured him. "The mother superior needs it to relieve her constipation."

Nodding with understanding, the man sold her the alcohol.

Later that day, when he went for lunch, the clerk was shocked to find the nun clinging to a streetlight, obviously drunk.

"My word!" he exclaimed. "You lied to me, Sister! You told me the vodka was for the mother superior's constipation!"

"I dinint lie," she protested. "When the mother superior sees me, she's gonna *shit!*"

3. Then there was the young man who left the priesthood after just two months. "Can you

imagine," he told a friend, "the torture of giving up your sex life only to have people come in and tell you the highlights of theirs?"

4. During a long sermon the little boy's eyes began to wander around the church. Spotting a plaque on the wall, he tugged his father's sleeve.

"Daddy," he whispered, "what's that for?"

"It's for all the men who died in the service," he said.

Growing pale, the boy asked, "Was Father Franklin giving the sermon then, too?"

5. When it was finally her turn to take care of the elderly Father Sands, the novice Jenny was taken aside by the mother superior.

"I must warn you," the older woman said, "that although Father Sands is old in body, he is young at heart. It is important that when you give him his bath, you never look below his waist. Otherwise, he will become very excited."

With that, Jenny went to look after the aged priest. Later, sobbing, Jenny sought out the mother superior.

"Forgive me," the novice said, "but when I was bathing Father Sands, I—I looked down. As you said, he became aroused."

"And what happened?"

"I—I lay with him. He said that I would surely go to heaven if I let him put his key to the gates of St. Peter in my lock."

"Why, that old bastard!" the mother superior fumed. "For years, he's been telling *me* it's Gabriel's trumpet!"

6. After listening to his roommate pontificate once again on religious splinter groups, one monk bellowed at the other, "Is that all you can think about? Sects! Sects! Sects!"

7. Then there was the priest who was notorious for his bad memory. Bumping into one of his flock at the grocery store, he couldn't, for the life of him, recall who she was.

"Good morning, Father O'Flannery," the woman said.

Smiling, the priest replied, "Forgive me, miss. I can't remember your name, but your faith is familiar."

---

**CLOTHING**　　　　*See also* BRASSIERES, HATS, SHOES, INSECTS 5, UNIONS 1, WORDPLAY 5

1. Though he loved the design of his new tie, Herman had no choice but to take it back to the store. When the clerk asked what was wrong with it, Herman said, "Too tight."

## COCKFIGHTS

1. Q: How can you tell if there's a Pole at a cockfight?
   A: He enters a canary.
   Q: How can you tell if there's an Iranian at a cockfight?
   A: He bets on the canary.
   Q: How can you tell if there's a Sicilian at a cockfight?
   A: The canary wins.


## COFFEE

*See also* TEA

1. After suffering through years of his wife's godawful coffee, the man spit it out and took the coffee maker to his lawyer. Dropping it on the attorney's desk, the man growled, "Here they are!"
   "Here are what?" the startled lawyer asked.
   "Grounds for divorce."


## COLLEGE

*See also* SCHOOL, ELEPHANTS 5, 6, 7, FOOTBALL 7, 8, INFIDELITY 11, REWARDS 2

1. The contractor was walking Mr. and Mrs. Brown through the house he was building for them. As the Browns told him what color they wanted the walls of the bedroom, the builder

ran over to the window and shouted, "Green side up!"

The threesome continued into the living room, where, as soon as the Browns told him the color they'd selected, the builder dashed to the window and yelled, "Green side up!"

When they reached the kitchen, the Browns were busy explaining what color appliances they wanted. Once again the builder darted to the window and hollered, "Green side up!"

"Say," Mr. Brown complained. "I'm getting sick and tired of this. Every time we tell you what color we want, you run off and scream, 'Green side up!' What's going on?"

"My apologies," the builder said, "but I hired a bunch of college kids to put down your lawn."

2. Q: What's the difference between a college professor and a proctologist?
   A: A proctologist only has to deal with one asshole at a time.

3. Today, of course, being college-bred means being a loaf for four years. . . .

## THE COMPLEXION

1. Q: What do husbands have in their pants that their wives don't want on their faces?
   A: Wrinkles.

1. Storming into the drugstore first thing Monday morning, the young man slammed a carton and a receipt down on the counter.

   "I came in here on Friday and purchased twelve dozen condoms," he yelled at the druggist. "Well, I counted them. There's only eleven dozen here."

   Regarding the man square in the eye, the druggist said contritely, "So sorry, sir, to have ruined your weekend."

2. Meanwhile, one canny entrepreneur sold his own brand of condom called Planned Parent Hood.

3. Q: What did the tampon say to the condom?
   A: "If you break, we're both unemployed!"

4. After having ten children, the Fermis decided they didn't want to have any more. Thus they went to the doctor for advice on birth control. He gave them a box of condoms, and told them that if they used them during sex, the chances were slim that they'd have any more children.

   Two months later, they were back in the doctor's office.

   "Well," said the physician, "I don't understand it, but Mrs. Fermi is pregnant again. Did you use the condoms like I told you?"

"You bet," said Mrs. Fermi. "We followed alla de instructions—except that since we no have de organ, I put it on de tambourine."

## CONFESSION    See also THE CLERGY, DRUNKS 1

1. While she was participating in the Olympics, the sixteen-year-old American gymnast had her first sexual experience, going to bed with a stunning East German.

   Upon returning to her hometown, she promptly went to confession. After receiving absolution, the gymnast was so delighted that she did cartwheels down the aisle to the door.

   Awaiting her turn, old Mrs. Willoughby said to her friend, "Can you believe what Father Pickmont is giving for penance? Of all the days for me not to be wearing panties. . . ."

2. Going to confession a young man said, "Father, forgive me, for I have sinned. I've had an affair with a woman who was not my wife."

   The priest said compassionately, "I understand. But to absolve you, I must have the name of the woman with whom you sinned."

   Reluctantly, the confessor said, "Her name is Pussy Pink. She's redheaded and *built*, Father. If you ever saw her, even you would understand!"

   The priest granted absolution, and the next Sunday he was watching from beside the organ as the congregation arrived for mass. Suddenly, a well-built redhead walked in. Nudging the organist, the priest said, "Mrs. Hyland, tell me—is that Pussy Pink?"

Looking behind her, the organist replied, "No, Father. It's just the sunlight passing through the stained-glass windows."

3. Ducking into confession with a turkey in his arms, the man said, "Forgive me, Father, for I have sinned. I stole this turkey to feed my family. Would you take it and assuage my guilt?"

"Certainly not," said the priest. "As penance, you must return it to the one from whom you stole it."

"I—I tried," the man sobbed, "but he refused. Oh, Father, what should I do?"

"If what you say is true, then it is all right for you to keep it for your family."

Thanking the priest, the man hurried off.

When confession was over, the priest returned to his residence. When he walked into the kitchen, he found that someone had stolen his Thanksgiving turkey.

## CONSTIPATION    See also BIRDS 4, CLERGY 2

1. Not that he wasn't grateful for the help, but the perpetually constipated Mr. Bloch took to referring to his doctor's office as "enema territory."

## COUNTRY SINGERS *See also* ROCK AND ROLL

1. Q: What did Johnny Cash end up with when he crossed an Indian with a black?

   A: A Sioux named Boy.

2. Nowadays, a country singer is someone who uses two million dollars worth of equipment to sing about the simple life.

## COURT-MARTIALS *See also* COURTROOMS, THE MILITARY

1. Colonel Lenny Wengler was arrested for running after a woman through a hotel lobby, both of them entirely naked. Brought up on charges, he got off on a technicality. As his lawyer pointed out, it is not necessary for an officer to be in uniform provided he is properly attired for the sport in which he's engaged.

## COURTROOMS *See also* COURT-MARTIALS, DIVORCE, LAWYERS, AUTHORS 1, CARTOON CHARACTERS 1

1. Returning home after a tour of the U.S., an Australian aborigine told his tribespeople about the strangest sight he had seen. "It was called a courtroom," he said. "And in it, one man sat silent, another was talking constantly, and when

it was over, twelve people ignored the one who was talking and condemned the man who hadn't said a word!"

2. A Russian visiting the U.S. was equally confused by the legal system. "It is most strange," he said. "At night it is the jury which is locked up, while the defendant is permitted to go home."

3. Also befuddled was a Chinese visitor who saw the following newspaper headline: "CRIMINAL EVADES NOOSE. JURY HUNG."

4. He also would have been confused by the two gay judges who decided to try each other.

5. Standing before the judge during an alimony hearing, the man said, "As God is my judge, I do not owe that madwoman money!"

The judge calmly replied, "He isn't. I am. You do."

6. Taking his seat in his chambers, the judge faced the opposing lawyers.

"So," he said, "I have been presented, by both of you, with a bribe."

Both lawyers squirmed uncomfortably.

"You, Attorney Papa, gave me $15,000. And you, Attorney Petroni, gave me $10,000." The judge reached into his robes and angrily pulled out a check. He handed it to Papa.

"Now then, I'm returning $5,000 and we're going to decide this case solely on its merits."

7. It was a heated trial, and after the defense's impassioned closing argument, the prosecutor rose indignantly.

"Mr. Andrews," he said, "I may be out of order, but everything you just said is utter hogwash."

Turning, the defense attorney calmly replied, "And you, Mr. Kenyon, are by far the most incredible *imbecile* I have ever known!"

"To the contrary!" Kenyon shot back. "It is you, sir, who can lay sole claim to that title!"

At which point the judge thumped his gavel and said, "Order! You gentlemen forget that *I'm* in the room!"

8. In a terrible accident at a railroad crossing, a train smashed into a car and pushed it nearly four hundred yards down the track. Though no one was killed, the driver took the train company to court.

At the trial, the engineer insisted that he had given the driver ample warning by waving his lantern back and forth for nearly a minute. He even stood and convincingly demonstrated how he'd done it. The court believed his story, and the suit was dismissed.

"Congratulations," the lawyer said to the engineer when it was over. "You did superbly under cross-examination."

"Thanks," he said, "but he sure had me worried."

"How's that?" the lawyer asked.

"I was afraid he was going to ask if the damned lantern was lit!'

9. In court to answer a paternity suit, eleven-year-old Ray stood at his lawyer's behest. To emphasize the spuriousness of the charge, the attorney unzipped the boy's pants and held his flaccid member.

"Ladies and gentlemen of the jury," the lawyer said, rattling the organ, "I ask you to study this undeveloped penis. Examine this limp, preadolescent genital and ask yourself, 'Is it possible that he could have fathered a baby with *this*!' "

Suddenly, from the corner of his mouth, Ray said, "Psst! Mr. Bigshot! If you don't let go real soon, we're gonna lose this case!"

10. Then there was the process server who became rather free-wheeling after years of puttin' on the writs. . . .


## COWS

*See also* BULLS, ABORTION 2

1. Q: What's a metaphor?
   A: So that livestock can graze.

2. Then there was the Polish farmer who didn't bother putting a bell on his cow, since she already had a pair of horns. . . .

3. By and large, cows are grateful beasts. They realize that all they have, they owe to udders.

## CRIME
*See also* COURT-MARTIALS, COURTROOMS, MURDER, PRISONS, HOMOSEXUALS 5, LANGUAGES 5, LAWYERS 5, 6

1. It was a bold crime: the thugs broke into the hat factory and stole nearly two hundred expensive fur hats. No surprise there, though, since the security guard was armed only with a cap gun. . . .

2. While Oscar was shopping for sporting goods, one of the salespeople came running up to him.
   "Oscar! Oscar! I just saw someone driving off with your Mercedes!"
   "Dear God! Did you try to stop him?"
   "No," said the clerk, "but don't worry. I got the license plate number!"

3. While strolling down Hollywood Boulevard at night, Wilson felt a gun pressed to the base of his head.
   "Gimme your money or I blow your brains out," a voice snarled from behind.

Without missing a beat Wilson said, "Go ahead and shoot. In Hollywood you can live without brains, but not without money."

4. After committing a daring bank robbery, the Polish bandits tore from the bank parking lot and sped onto the turnpike.

"Karel," said the driver, "look back and see if the cops are following us."

"How will I know?" the other asked.

"He'll have his flashers on, dammit!"

Karel looked back. After peering through the window for several moments, he answered, "Yes . . . no . . . yes . . . no . . . yes. . . ."

5. Q: When the victim was brought into the room, what did the Pole in the police lineup say?

   A: "That's the woman!"

## CRITICS                          *See also* AUTHORS

1. Having lunch with one of his business authors, the editor gingerly brought up the subject of the review in the *Times*.

"So," he said, "do you know what Eric had to say about your stock market book?"

The woman shook her head. "I have no idea whatsoever."

The editor replied, "Well . . . more or less."

2. At the publishing party, the novelist cornered the famous literary critic.

   "So tell me, what did you think of my new book? Your opinions carry a lot of weight, you know."

   The critic sniffed. "The truth is, it's without merit."

   Replied the novelist, "Oh, I know. But I'd love to hear it just the same."

3. Discovering a long-lost review of Shakespeare's acting career, a scholar was gratified to note that critics have always been an acerbic bunch. Commenting on the playwright's transition from author to actor, the critic noted simply, "He has gone from bard to voice."

4. Then there was the doctor-turned-literary-critic who was having lunch with a first-time novelist. When the check arrived, the critic grabbed it.

   "This is mine," he insisted, "I've always treated neuritis."

5. It was a dying art, so clockmaster Hans Pfall decided to write a book about his craft. When it was published, all the critics said it was about time.

## CRUISES

See also TOURISTS

1. Adler was so nervous about the cruise that immediately after being shown to her cabin, she headed for the bar.

   Four hours later, she bumped into a steward.

   " 'Scuse me," she said, hiccuping, "I—I can't seem to find my cabin."

   "I'll be glad to help you, ma'am. What's the number?"

   "I dunno," she answered, "but if you show me aroun', I'll recognize it from the lighthouse just outside the porthole."

## CRYOGENICS

1. Q: What do cryogenicists sing when interring each new subject?
   A: "Freeze a jolly good fellow!"

## DATING

See also ENGAGEMENTS, PROPOSALS, SEX, EPILEPTICS 1, THE FOREIGN LEGION 1, INSECTS 1, JOAN OF ARC 1, SEX 16, 17, TOBACCO 1

1. While nursing a drink at a bar, a young woman was distressed to see a drunken, unkempt man sit down next to her.

   "Say, honey-baby . . . I'd really like t'get into those pants o'yours."

"Thanks," she shot back, "but I've already got an asshole in there."

2. Two young women were cruising the singles' bars, but were unsuccessful at finding a man. Finally, at the last bar in town they spotted a single fellow sitting at the bar.

One of the girls walked over to him. "You don't look very happy," she said.

"I'm not. I've just spent fifteen years in prison."

"Fifteen years! What for?"

"I beat my wife unconscious with a baseball bat, then threw her into a wood chipper."

Nodding, the girl looked back at her friend and yells, "He's single!"

3. Strolling through a singles' bar, Mr. Hampton spotted a lovely young woman sitting alone at a table, and walked over.

"Say, babe, how about coming along and giving me a little head?"

The woman looked up. "That'll be the day."

Undaunted, the man said, "Well then, how about coming along to my apartment and screwing?"

Snickering, the woman said, "That'll be the day!"

"Okay," said the man. "How about taking my limo to my private jet, flying to Tahiti, and spending the weekend on my private beach?"

The woman said, "This'll be the day."

4. Sitting around the breakfast table, Sam turned to his brother Michael and said, "You know what Judy told me last night in the car?"

   "No."

   Sam frowned. "Hey—you were listening!"

5. Then there was the businessperson who told a nervous client to think of her computer-matchup service simply as dater-processing.

6. Q: What's the major difference between men and women?

   A: Women must play hard to get. . . .

7. Every night before she went out on a date, the young girl was told by her mother, "Remember, dear. When he tries to touch you a certain way, a girl's best friends are her legs."

   Much to her mother's dismay, however, several weeks later her daughter announced that she was pregnant.

   "What! How did it happen? Didn't I tell you that your best friends are your legs?"

   "You did, Mama," she replied. "But there comes a time when even best friends must part."

8. When his teenage son asked to borrow twenty dollars, the man said, "Son, don't you realize that there are more important things in life than money?"

"Yes, sir," the youth replied, "I do. But you've got to have money to take them to the movies."

9. Approaching the woman at a singles' bar, the young man said, "Hi, cookie. How about a date?"

"Forget it," she said. "I never go out with perfect strangers."

"We're both in luck," he said. "I'm far from perfect."

10. Old Mr. Weisinger lay badly dehydrated in a hospital bed. Because his jaw was broken and the veins in his arms were too small, he was being fed rectally.

After a few days he began to regain his strength. Spotting a beautiful young nurse fluffing his pillow, he pointed to a pad of paper and wrote her a note.

"Listen," he scribbled, "I think you're very lovely. Why don't you bring another tube when you get off work, and we'll have dinner together?"

**DEATH**    *See also* EXECUTIONS, MURDER, REINCARNATION, ACTORS 1, FOOTBALL 6, 12, FORTUNE-TELLERS 1, SEX 19

1. Attending the funeral of an actress who had been married ten times, a friend sobbed to

the priest, "Well . . . at least they're together at last."

The clergyman looked around. "Which of her husbands is buried here?"

"None," said the friend. "I meant, her legs."

2. "I have good news and I have bad news," Dr. Franklin told his old friend Costello.

"Let me have the bad news first," Costello said bravely.

"Well, my friend, I'm afraid your illness is terminal. You have only a year to live."

"Dear God," Costello said, then forced a smile. "T-tell me, doc, what's the good news?"

"When you came in, did you see the receptionist with the huge tits? I'm fucking her brains out."

**DEFECATION**                    *See also* FLATULENCE,
                            LAVATORIES, SEPTIC TANKS,
                    AIRPLANES 1, LIONS 2, LITERATURE 3

1. While hunting, the moron told his friend he had to move his bowels.

"Go behind the tree," the friend said. "No one'll see you there."

"And what do I use to wipe myself?" the moron asked.

"Use a dollar," said the friend. "It'll scratch less than if you use leaves."

A few minutes later, the moron returned; there was shit all over his hand.

"Say," the friend said, "what's with the hands? I thought I told you to use a dollar."

"I did," said the moron. "You should see how dirty the quarters are!"

## THE DEFICIT
See also BANKING, BANKRUPTCY, THE STOCK MARKET, PRESIDENTS 2

1. This administration has conclusively discovered how to deal with the deficit. It's a skill which requires addition and distraction.

2. Yet, still the president insists the economy is in good shape. As one of his spokespeople put it, "Sure it's fit! Look how fast money goes!"

3. The same president also swears that the economy is bouncing back. What he doesn't reveal is the reason: the fact that most checks today are made of rubber.

4. As for money, it's only called cold cash nowadays because it doesn't stay in your pocket long enough to get warm.

1. Mrs. Goldblatt wasn't keen on having her tooth pulled, but the dentist assured her there was no other choice. Nonetheless, every time he went to put the forceps in her mouth, she clenched her teeth.

   Whispering to the nurse, the dentist tried again. At the instant he approached her, the nurse pinched Mrs. Goldblatt's side with all her strength. The woman's mouth opened wide, and the tooth was pulled.

   "Now," the dentist said when it was all over, "that wasn't so bad."

   "No," Mrs. Goldblatt agreed, "but who'd have imagined that the roots went so far down!"

2. Sitting down in the dentist's chair, Mrs. Hart grew pale.

   "I honestly don't know what's worse," she said, "having my teeth drilled or having a baby."

   The dentist stood back. "Well, make up your mind," he said, "so I'll know which way to tilt the chair."

1. After examining an overweight patient, the doctor prescribed a diet. "At your age," the physician said, "you have to be careful that you don't put too great a strain on your heart. So whatever you do, don't give up on this." He handed him the prescription and said, "A month from now, I want to see three-quarters of you back here for a checkup."

2. Terribly overweight, Don LaJoie went to the doctor and begged him to be put on a diet. The doctor suggested several, but Lajoie rejected them all, insisting that he had no willpower.

   Considering the problem, the doctor said, "There is one thing we can try. It's an experimental diet in which the jaw is wired shut and nourishment is provided through the rectum. Since the rectal walls can only absorb small amounts of food at a time, you will lose weight quickly."

   LaJoie agreed to try the diet. Three weeks later, he returned for his checkup and, much to the doctor's delight, the formerly obese man was now quite slender. He also had a remarkable bounce to his step.

   The physician removed the wire from LaJoie's jaw and the man sat down. Much to the doctor's surprise, his patient continued to bounce up and down on the seat.

"So how do you feel?" the doctor asked.

"Marvelous! Never better."

"Then tell me, why are you bouncing up and down like that?"

"Oh," says LaJoie, "I'm just chewing some gum."

## DIPLOMATS

See also THE IRISH 1

1. At a United Nations cocktail party, the Mexican ambassador walked over to a group of his colleagues.

   "Pardon me," he said, "but what is your opinion of the meat shortage?"

   The American scratched his head. "What's a shortage?"

   The Pole frowned. "What's meat?"

   The Russian shrugged. "What's an opinion?"

   And the Israeli demanded, "What's 'pardon me'?"

## DISEASES

See also EPILEPTICS, LEPERS, ACUPUNCTURE 1, NUCLEAR ACCIDENTS 2, PROSTITUTES, VIRGINITY 2, WORDPLAY 4

1. When Moe went to the doctor, the GP's face was unusually long.

   "I don't know how it happened," the physician said, "but we got your test results mixed up with those of someone else. Either you've got Alzheimer's disease . . . or AIDS."

"My God!" Moe slapped his cheek, "that's terrible. What should I do?"

"All I can suggest," said the doctor, "is that if you find your way home, do *not* screw your wife."

2. Q: How did the hemorrhoid sufferer know that the Preparation H was working?
   A: After weeks of pain he was finally able to just sit back and watch the tube.

3. Then there was the outbreak of a tragic new malady: Waldheimer's Disease. People who suffer from it forget that they were ever Nazis.

## DIVORCE

See also MARRIAGE, COFFEE 1, COURTROOMS 5

1. Storming into his lawyer's office, a Texas oil magnate demanded that divorce proceedings begin at once against his young bride.

   "What's the problem?"

   "I want to hit that adulterin' bitch for breach of contract," snapped the oil man.

   "I don't know if that'll fly," said the lawyer. "I mean, your wife isn't a piece of property, you don't *own* her—"

   "Damn right," the tycoon rejoined, "but I sure as hell expect exclusive drillin' rights!"

2. "I don't understand it," the judge said. "Mrs. Collins, you say in your complaint that you want a divorce due to poor health and exhaustion. Explain."

"It's simple, Your Honor," said the woman. "I'm sick and tired of having that bastard around."

3. The lawyers were interviewing prospective jurists, and it was Mrs. Finkelstein's turn.

"No," she said, "I don't think I can serve. You see, I do not believe in capital punishment."

"Madam," said one attorney, "this isn't a case of homicide. A man is being sued by his wife. They were in Atlantic City. She gave him twenty thousand dollars to buy her a mink coat, and he gambled it away at the casino."

Mrs. Finkelstein said without hesitation, "I'll serve. I could be wrong about capital punishment."

4. "So, Ms. Allen," said the judge, "you wish me to grant you a divorce. On what grounds?"

"Two acres," she said.

The judge frowned. "I mean, do you have a grudge?"

"Yes sir," she answered. "Fits two cars."

"Madam, what I mean is—does he beat you up?"

"Never. I get up half an hour before him to do aerobics."

Shaking his head, the judge said, "I just can't understand why you want a divorce!"

"Because," the woman complained, "we just don't communicate!"

5. Then there was the sage who pointed out that "alimony" is simply a contraction of "all his money."

6. Another sage described alimony as the bounty on the mutiny.

7. To put it yet another way, alimony is that which marks a man's transition from a co-starring part to a supporting role.

**DOCTORS**    *See also* DENTISTS, DIETS, DISEASES, GYNECOLOGISTS, MEDICAL SCHOOL, PEDIATRICIANS, PODIATRISTS, PSYCHIATRISTS, SPERM BANKS, SURGERY, X RAYS, ACTORS 2, AMNESIA 2, RACQUETBALL 1, CARDS 1, 2, DRUGS 1, DRUNKS 3, GOLF 1, LANGUAGES 4, LEPERS 1, NYMPHOMANIACS 4, SPEECH IMPEDIMENTS 1, VENEREAL DISEASES 1, 2, WILLS 1, WORDPLAY 11, 14

1. While having lunch in Central Park, a pair of retired doctors saw a man walking their way. His knees were pressed together, his hands were clenched in tight fists, and his wrists were bent inward, toward his waist.

"You still got your knack for diagnosin'?" asked one doctor.

"Sure. Why?"

He gestured toward the man. "I'd say that poor fellow's got cerebral palsy."

The other doctor shook his head. "Arthritis, for sure."

"Let's find out," said the first.

However, before the doctor could ask, the man stopped in front of their bench. He said through his teeth, "Pardon me, but do either of you gentlemen know where in this damn park the rest rooms are?"

2. During his annual checkup, Mr. Ellis said to his physician, "Doctor . . . my biggest trouble is that I can't pee."

The doctor stroked his chin. "How old are you?"

"Ninety-two," Mr. Ellis replied.

"What are you complaining for?" asked the doctor. "Haven't you peed enough?"

3. While visiting his physician for an annual checkup, Mr. Morton was surprised when the doctor told him to strip, go to the window, and wave his exposed genitals in the fresh air.

While doing as the doctor had asked, Mr. Morton asked, "Just what is this going to tell you?"

"Not a thing," the doctor answered. "I happen to hate my neighbors."

4. Though it had never happened before, Dr. Jones was so smitten with his lovely if naive young patient, Mrs. Smith, that he had to have her. Telling her that he needed to take her temperature, he took his penis in hand and slipped it inside her.

Just then Mr. Smith walked in. "Hey!" he yelled. "What the hell do you think you're doing?"

Dr. Jones muttered, "Taking your wife's temperature, of course."

Mr. Smith grabbed a scalpel from the cabinet. "Okay, Jones," he said. "But when you pull that thing out, there damn well better be numbers on it."

5. While waiting for her husband to finish up with his last patient, Mrs. O'Leary looked up from a magazine just as a little girl came running from the office. Her face was buried in her hands, and she was sobbing terribly.

"Josh," the woman said when she went in to see her husband, "why was that girl so distraught?"

"I told her she was going to have a baby," the doctor replied.

"What! But she's only eight or nine years old! How could that be?"

"It can't," the doctor admitted. "But it sure as hell cured her hiccups."

6. "Doc," the patient asked, "is it okay to file my nails?"

"Sure," the doctor replied, "but why don't you throw them out like everyone else?"

7. "Dr. Gish," said the woman in a very deep voice, "I—I hate to say it, but I think you overdid it on the hormone pills."

"Don't worry," the doctor assured her. "A deep voice is a natural development. It'll only last a few days."

"But I've also sprouted hair on my chest," she said.

"Really? And how far down does it reach."

She replied, "All the way to my balls."

8. Q: How many doctors does it take to screw in a light bulb?
   A: It depends on whether or not the bulb has health insurance.

9. Dr. Phelps had known many interns during his long career, but none ever made as many misdiagnoses as young Clayton. After making the rounds one day, and watching him make a dozen wrong diagnoses on a dozen patients, Phelps finally took the intern aside.

"Tell me," the doctor asked, "have you ever considered working somewhere else?"

"Where, for instance?"

Phelps replied, "Wall Street?"

10. Q: What is it that a swan can do with ease, a duck can manage with a bit of effort,

and a doctor should most definitely do?

A: Stick his bill up his ass.

11. Feeling dizzy and nauseous, Sam went to the doctor.

   "So," said the physician as Sam sat on the examining table, "what seems to be wrong?"

   At once Sam shot to his feet, grabbed his hat and coat, and stormed toward the door.

   "What's the matter?" the doctor demanded.

   "The nerve of you!" Sam snapped. "All those years of medical school, and you want *me* to make the diagnosis!"

12. Exhausted by long, tense months of work, Dr. Denton decides to unwind by going on a safari. When he returns, his nurse asks him how he enjoyed himself.

   "It was terrible," he said, "I didn't kill a thing. Frankly, I'd have been better off staying here."

13. According to the sage, an internist knows everything and does nothing, a surgeon does everything and knows nothing, and a psychiatrist knows nothing and does nothing. Only a pathologist knows everything and does everything . . . too late.

14. Which brings us to specialists, who are doctors that know more and more about less and less. . . .

## DOGS

*See also* CATS, BIRDS 3, CHILDBIRTH 1, REWARDS 1, SENIOR CITIZENS 3

1. Much to his surprise, a farmer was out in the field one morning when a dog came ambling by, singing a song. Realizing that he could make a fortune with a talking dog, he said, "Hey, today's February 12. Why don't we go to town and bet people that you can tell them whose birthday it is."

   The dog was amenable, and they climbed into the farmer's truck. At the local diner he bet everyone five dollars that he could get the dog to tell them who was born on this day. However, much to the farmer's chagrin, the dog just sat there.

   On the way back to the farm the man said, "I ought to whip the tar outta you. Ya cost me nearly $200 back there!"

   "It's nothing," said the dog. "Think of the odds we're gonna get on Washington's Birthday."

2. Due to the high cost of beef, the Orientals have come up with a new concept in eating: wokking the dog.

3. After hearing a shot, Todd ran next door and found his friend Jason crying.

   "Say, what's wrong?"

   Todd sobbed, "I—I just had to shoot my dog."

   "My God! Was he mad?"

   "Well," said Todd, "he wasn't exactly thrilled."

4. Q: What does a dog do that a person steps in?
   A: Pants.

5. While driving through the south, tourists Jane and Joe stopped into a country store for candy. While they were paying, they noticed a group of men playing cards with a poodle.

   Joe said to the clerk, "Can that dog really play cards?"

   "Yet bet."

   "That's incredible!"

   "Not really," the clerk shrugged.

   "Not really?"

   "Naw, he ain't as bright as all that. Whenever he gets a good hand, he wags his tail."

6. Then there was the dog who went to the flea circus and stole the show. . . .

7. After placing an ad for an assistant who could work a word processor, take dictation, and speak more than one language, an office manager was stunned when a dog applied for the job.

She was even more surprised when, showing the dog to the computer, it was able to create files, type in letters and documents, and even write its own programs. What's more, the animal took dictation better than any assistant the woman had ever seen.

"Well," said the office manager, "I'm impressed. Now, what about the language requirement?"

Sitting back in its chair, the dog said, "Meow."

8. Q: What's the difference between a mangy dog and a dead bee?
   A: One's a seedy beast. . . .

9. Farmer Scott boasted to his friend Jason that he owned a dog that could count. Jason told Scott to prove it, and to make things more interesting, he suggested that they put a wager on it. Scott agreed and, calling the dog, the farmer, his friend, and the animal headed to the barn.

"How many cows we got here?" Scott asked the dog.

The dog looked around, then ran in a circle three times.

"Three cows," the farmer said. "He's right."

Jason still wasn't convinced, and suggested they go somewhere the dog didn't frequent. Walking out to a pond nearly a mile away, the farmer asked the dog how many ducks were on the water.

The dog studied the pond for several seconds, then ran a circle five times. Sure enough, there were five ducks on the pond.

Wanting one more example before paying up, Jason asked the dog to tell him how many squirrels were in a nearby tree.

The dog studied the old oak. All of a sudden, he began humping Scott's leg, then picked up a branch and started swinging it back and forth.

"Hah!" the friend said. "Just as I thought! That dog's dumber than toast."

"Like hell," said Scott. "What he's sayin' is that there are more fucking squirrels than you can shake a stick at."


**THE DRAFT**   *See also* THE MILITARY, MASTURBATION 2

1. Called up in the draft, Jed and Judd had no desire to serve in the army. Thus they had all their teeth yanked out, aware that the military wouldn't take them if they were toothless.

   Showing up for their exam, they were lined up along with a burly man.

   When Jed stepped up to the doctor, the physician said, "Anything wrong with you?"

   "Yes sir," Jed replied, "I have no teeth."

   Pushing his fingers into Jed's mouth, the doctor felt around. "Right," he said, "you're 4F."

The doctor called over the big man next. "Anything wrong with you?"

"Yeah," he said, "I got piles."

Reaching around, the doctor pushed his fingers into the man's anus. "You sure do, you're 4F."

Judd was summoned. "Anything wrong with you?"

"Not a thing," Judd replied.

## DRUGS

See also SEX 1

1. It was the day the players dreaded: testing for drugs in their systems. Sending a nurse to get samples from the players, the doctor decided to go to the locker room and see how things were progressing. He was horrified by what he saw.

   "No, you idiot!" he screamed. "I told you to *prick* their *fingers!*"

2. Then there were the basketball players who were busted for cocaine use. Naturally, they hired crack attorneys.

3. And what about the Mets pitcher who gave up walk after walk because he loved freebasing. . . .

**DRUNKS**

*See also* CEMETERIES 1, CLERGY 2, CRUISES 1, FISH 1, THE IRISH 1, LAVATORIES 1, LOGIC 4, MUSIC 4, PIGS 1, POVERTY 1

1. Drunk and with no idea where he was, McKay walked into a church and stumbled into a confessional.

   Moments after he sat down, there was a tap on the partition. Looking through, McKay said, "Forget it! I ain't got no paper in here *either!*"

2. The desk sergeant answered the phone, and a man, obviously drunk, began screaming at him. "It's terrible! I went into the bar for a few drinks, and when I came out they'd ransacked my car! They took the radio, the steering wheel, the brake, the gas pedal, the glove compartment—the whole friggin' dashboard, in fact!"

   After dutifully writing down the address of the bar, the desk sergeant dispatched a car. Moments later, the phone rang again.

   "Never mind," the drunk told him. "I got in the backseat by mistake."

3. Dr. Reynolds was disgusted when Don staggered into her office, thoroughly inebriated.

   She looked at him sternly. "What happened, Don? I thought we were going to lick this problem by cutting you down to just two drinks a day."

Don dragged a finger across his chest. "Cross my heart, doc, I—I did as y'asked."

"Impossible. If you had, you wouldn't be in this shape."

"No, honestly!" Don replied. "In fact, when I left here the other day, I went to another doctor for a second opinion—and he prescribed the same thing!"

4. Conferring with a friend on the street corner, the drunk said, "Y'know, I'll never forget the first time I turned to the bottle as a substitute for women."

"Why?" said the friend. "What happened?"

The drunk replied, "I got my dong stuck in the bottle."

5. Managing to pull himself onto the bus early one morning, the drunk stumbled over passengers, knocked over bags and briefcases, and finally fell into a seat beside a prim old woman. He slumped over on her, and she pushed him back.

"Mister," she said indignantly. "I hate to say it, but you're going straight to hell!"

Startled, the drunk leapt to his feet. "Christ, I'm on the wrong bus!"

6. After several hours the man at the bar was so drunk that he began to slump over onto the people beside him. In no uncertain terms the bartender told him that he'd had enough and had to leave.

"Had 'nuff, huh?" the man said. Noticing a cat walking across the room, he said, "I can *prove* I isn't drunk. See that cat comin' inna door? Well, she only has one eye."

"You're drunk, all right," the bartender said. "That cat's leaving."

7. "Shay," said the drunk to the bartender, "do lemons have wings?"

"Don't be ridiculous," the bartender replied.

"Then I'm sorry."

"Why?"

" 'Cause I just squeezed your canary into my drink."


## EASTER                        *See also* SEX 28, 29

1. Knock, knock.
Who's there?
Esther.
Esther who?
The Esther Bunny.

Knock, knock.
Who's there?
Stella.
Stella who?
Stella nother Esther Bunny.

Knock, knock.
Who's there?

Samoa
Samoa who?
Samoa Esther bunnies.

Knock, knock.
Who's there?
Consumption.
Consumption who?
Consumption be done about all these Esther Bunnies?

Knock, knock.
Who's there?
Esther.
Esther who?
Esther anyone else as sick of this joke as I am?

2. While out for a stroll around the farm on Easter morning, Mr. Rooster happened to spot a pile of vividly colored eggs. Growing livid, the fowl rushed into the woods and beat the living shit out of Mr. Peacock.

## ECOLOGY

1. Fearing the worst, the ecologist began a campaign to control water pollution. "Otherwise," she told the newspapers, "this nation is going to go from one ex-stream to another."

1. Sick and tired of his friend Stan, who was constantly name-dropping and boasting of how famous he was, Larry said, "If you're such a big shot, you'll go over to the phone, call the White House, and get the president on the line."

   Shrugging, Stan walked to the phone, punched in a number, and handed the receiver to Larry.

   "Hello," came a familiar voice. "This is the president speaking."

   Convinced it was a fluke, Larry said, "Okay, that was impressive—but if you're *really* a hotshot, you'll call Buckingham Palace and let me talk to the queen."

   With a bored sigh Stan went back to the phone, punched in a number, and gave the receiver to Larry.

   "Hello," came a distinctive voice. "This is the Queen of England speaking."

   *Very* impressed, but still suspicious, Larry said, "All right, you happen to know the president and the queen. But if you're *really* a big deal, you'll get the pope on the phone."

   Promising to do better than that, Stan took Larry to the airport and both men boarded a plane to the Vatican. There, Stan disappeared, leaving Larry to mill about with the crowd in St. Peter's Square.

   Suddenly the crowd fell into a reverent silence. Larry followed their gaze to a balcony, where Stan and the pope stood side by side.

Before Larry could recover from his amazement, a man standing beside him poked him in the ribs.

"Hey," he asked, "who's that up there with Stan?"

2. Then there was the actor who was so conceited that on his birthday he sent his parents flowers and a note of congratulations.

3. Jim happened to bump into his friend Gary at the tennis club. "So," Jim said, "how's it working out with that shrink I recommended."

"Great," Gary said. "I mean, when I started, I was the most arrogant, self-impressed egomaniac on God's green earth. Now," he shrugged, "you couldn't ask to meet a more terrific guy than me."

4. Then there was the egotist who wrote a love letter: I.

5. . . . And the two raving egomaniacs who met at a party and ended up trading an I for an I. . . .

1. The desk sergeant answered the phone, and at once a woman began screaming.

   "You've got to help me! There's a giant gray thing in my front yard, and it's pulling apples off the tree with its tail!"

   "What's he doing with the apples?" the sergeant asked.

   "If I told you," the woman cried, "you wouldn't believe me!"

2. Q: How do you get down from an elephant?
   A: You don't. You get down from a goose.

3. Q: What do you get when you cross an elephant and a prostitute?
   A: A half-ton pickup.

4. Q: What did the elephant say when he saw the native warrior running naked through the jungle?
   A: "How the hell does he *eat* with that thing?"

5. "It's common knowledge," said the zoology
   student, "that elephants have their genitals in their feet."

   "Really?" said the professor.

   "Absolutely," smiled the pupil. "If they step on you, you're fucked."

6. "Not only that," the student went on, "but I've discovered that elephants and my digital watch have something in common."

"And what is that?" enquired the teacher.

"They both come in quartz."

7. "And I suppose," the budding zoologist continued doggedly, "that you don't know why elephants have four feet."

The teacher smiled. "Because six inches won't satisfy lady elephants?"

8. While taking a long drink at a pond, an elephant happened to glance up and spotted a snapping turtle lazing on a nearby stone. Its eyes narrowing, the elephant lumbered over, raised a foot, and pressed the turtle flat.

Observing the murder from the jungle, a zebra wandered over.

"Why the heck did you do that?"

"This was the same animal that bit off the tip of my trunk over ten years ago."

The zebra's eyes widened. "The same one? You must have an incredible memory!"

Raising its head proudly, the elephant said, "Turtle recall."

1. After years in the work force, someone finally concluded that an employer is someone who's late when you're early, and early when you're late. . . .

2. . . . Someone who's also known as the crank which turns the wheels of progress.

3. Worse, though, than the cruel employer is the office bootlicker, someone who stoops to concur. . . .

4. The sad truth, though, is the fact that the work ethic isn't what it used to be: required.

5. Goldberg got into the elevator and saw Malcolm, his delivery boy, grinning.

"And what are you so happy about?" Goldberg asked.

"TGIF!" the boy crowed. "Thank God It's Friday!"

"Shit."

Malcolm looked at him. "Shit? How can you say that on such a great day."

"I can say that because of SHIT! So Happens It's Thursday. . . ."

6. Then there was poor Jackson, who was with the automobile manufacturer for less than a month when he was fired for taking a brake.

## ENGAGEMENTS

*See also* DATING, MARRIAGE, PROPOSALS

1. After Bernice told her friend Cindy about her engagement to old man Whittaker, Cindy shuddered.

   "Sorry," the woman said, "but there's no way I'd marry him. Everyone in town knows that he's cracked!"

   "Cracked he may be," Bernice agreed, "but he sure as hell ain't broke."

2. Discussing her fiancé with a friend, the young Mexican girl said, "Pedro wasn't really my first choice, you know."

   "No? I thought he was a very nice man."

   "Oh, he is," said the girl. "But you should have seen the Juan that got away."

3. And it was barely two days after Clarence got engaged to the circus contortionist that she broke it off. . . .

**ENTREPRENEURS**     *See also* BUSINESS, CONDOMS 2, SEX TOYS 2

1. After years of working for others and being passed over for promotions, Ken and his wife, Loree, decided to go into business together. After examining the classifieds, they bought a small candy stand, paying forty cents for each box of candy and then selling it for forty cents.

   At the end of the day they were astonished to find that they had sold every box of candy—yet had exactly as much money as when they started.

   "You see?" Ken snarled at his wife. "I *told* you we should've bought a larger stand!"

**EPILEPTICS**     *See also* DISEASES

1. Q: What's the most dangerous aspect of dating an epileptic woman?
   A: She could very well swallow *your tongue*, *too!*

**ESKIMOS**     *See also* JOAN OF ARC 2

1. Horny after a long hunt, the Eskimo returned to town, dropped into the local brothel, and asked for a nose job.

2. Unfortunately for the horny Eskimo, all but one of the women were taken. And *she* wouldn't touch him, being a Klondyke.

3. Finally, though, the frustrated Eskimo *did* find a woman with whom to spend the night. However, when morning came, she was six months pregnant.

4. Freezing while they were fishing, a pair of Eskimos decided to light a fire in the bottom of their kayak. But their joy was short-lived as just a minute after they started the blaze, the boat sank. Moral: You can't have your kayak and heat it, too.

## ETIQUETTE

1. While eating at a local diner, Mr. and Mrs. Everson exchange horrified glances as the trucker sitting next to them lets out an enormous belch.

   Tapping him indignantly on the shoulder, Mr. Everson says, "How dare you belch like that before my wife!

   Looking up from his soup, the trucker says, "Sorry. I didn't know it was her turn."

1. While watching a televangelist, an aged couple were stirred when he exclaimed, "God will *heal* you! Rise . . *rise* and put one hand on the TV, the other on whatever part of you is ailing!"

   The old woman rose slowly, placed one hand on the TV and the other on her bent, arthritic elbow. The old man stood unsteadily and put one hand on the TV, the other on his crotch.

   The old woman sneered. "Dammit, Amos, the preacher said that God would heal the sick, not raise the dead!"

2. Q: What is the holiest of all tomes to a TV evangelist?
   A: The pocket book.

## EVOLUTION

1. Q: How many evolutionists does it take to screw in a light bulb?
   A: Just one, but it takes him 200,000 years.

1. During the Second World War, a Briton, a Frenchman, and a Pole were captured by the Germans. Each man was sentenced to stand before a firing squad.

   The Briton was the first to be put against the wall. Standing back, the German *oberst* said, "Ready, aim—"

   At which point the Briton interrupted by shouting *"Earthquake!"*

   The firing squad ran for cover, and the Briton escaped.

   Regrouping, the Germans put the Frenchman against the wall. Once again the *oberst* said, "Ready, aim—"

   *"Flood!"* Taking a leaf from the Briton's book, the Frenchman yelled.

   Once again the Germans panicked, and the prisoner escaped.

   Finally the Polish resistance fighter faced the guns, ready to repeat the ploy of his predecessors. The *oberst* said, "Ready, aim—"

   *"Fire!"* hollered the Pole.

2. Murray, Steve, and Ryan were found guilty of first-degree murder and sentenced to die by electrocution.

   While he was being strapped into the chair, Murray, an accountant, offered to keep the state's books free of charge for the rest of his life if the governor would grant a stay. His offer was refused and the lever was thrown. However, nothing happened, and, by law, Murray was set free.

Steve, a cook, offered to make a gourmet lunch for the top government officials every day for as long as he lived if they let him go. But once again the sentence was carried out—and once again the criminal was released.

Ryan, an electrician, was led to the chair. While he was strapped in, he said to the guards, "Listen, if you let me go, I'll tell you that this thing won't work until you go around back and reconnect the white wire to the red one. . . ."

3. During the American Revolution, Martha Goode was arrested by the British and found guilty of using her sexual wiles for the purpose of spying. She was sentenced to be hanged.

While the executioner was busy fastening the noose around her neck, he couldn't help but let his eyes rove. "You know," he said, "you've got an incredible body."

Never one to give up, Martha replied, "You can have it, too, if you just keep your trap shut!"

4. "I've got good news and bad news," the lawyer said to his client, a convicted killer.

"What's the bad news?"

"They're still going to electrocute you at sunrise."

"Jesus Christ! Then what's the good news?"

The lawyer smiled proudly. "I got the voltage reduced."

5. It was a miserable day when the Panamanian dissident was walked from his prison to the distant field where he was to be shot. The firing squad marched behind him, rain pouring down upon them, mud sloshing into their boots.

When the prisoner was put up against the wall, the sergeant asked if he had anything to say.

"Yes," said the prisoner. "It is unfair that I must die!"

"What the hell are you complaining about?" the sergeant sneered. "*We're* the ones who have to walk back in this weather!"

6. On the morning of his execution Grant was visited by the chaplain.

"They are going to allow you ten minutes of grace," he said.

The prisoner shrugged. "That ain't very long, but what the hell. Send her in."

7. Then there was the gay murderer who was sent to the electric chair and blew a fuse.

## EXHIBITIONISTS

*See also* SEX,
FOOTBALL 2, WEATHER 1

1. Told by his psychiatrist to stop spending all his time reading pornography and to expose himself to real art, the perpetually horny young man took his advice. Traveling to the Louvre, he opened his trench coat in front of the *Mona Lisa*.

2. Far from cured, the exhibitionist got himself arrested at Burger King: he drove to the take-out window and did so.

## EXPENSE ACCOUNTS

1. Returning to work after attending the book-sellers' convention, the publicist turned in her expense account. It was kicked back by the head of accounting with the following memo: "Can't approve this expense account. Suggest, though, that you talk to editorial about buying the fiction rights."

## EXTRATERRESTRIALS

1. Landing in Las Vegas, a Plutonian walked into a casino. While he's observing the partrons, he noticed a slot machine spit out a flood of silver dollars.

Walking over when the customer had left, the alien said to the machine, "You're silly not to be home with a cold like that!"

2. Walking through the city, a pair of Jovians noticed a snappy little sportscar. "You know," said one, "I think I'll take that back to Jupiter with us."

   "Watch it," warned the other, "she may be underage."

3. While strolling along Main Street, a Venusian female stopped and looked longingly into the window of a paint store. The Venusian at her side stopped and sighed.

   "I'm sorry," he said, "but your old coat will just have to last you another year."

4. After being spirited away onboard a flying saucer, an earth couple was confronted by its blob-like occupant.

   The aliens interviewed the earth people, asking them about politics, culture, religion, and diet. Finally one blob said, "We're through, except for one thing. We would like very much for you to show us how little earthlings are conceived."

   Since they were in no position to refuse, the couple disrobed and made love. When they'd finished, the blob's five eyes continued to look on dispassionately.

   "Is that all?" the creature asked.

"Yes," the earth woman said. "What's wrong?"

"I must tell you, I'm very disappointed."

"Why?"

The alien said, "Because that's how *we* manufacture VCRs."

5. Still not sure they understood human reproductive activity, the aliens kidnapped another couple and asked them to mate so they could observe the procedure.

When they were finished, one extraterrestrial said, "And how long does it take for the new earthling to arrive?"

"About nine months," replied the woman.

The alien scratched its head. "If that is so, then why were you in such a hurry at the end?"

6. For its part, the other extraterrestrial was concerned with a different problem. "Never mind the hurry. If it takes nine earth months, then why did you stop stirring?"

7. While strolling through a field one day, Milton was shocked as a flying saucer settled into the grass not far away. Running over, he watched with awe as a door slid back and an alien strode out. The visitor, who looked not unlike a human, approached Milton.

After they exchanged greetings, the terrestrial said, "My word, it's incredible! A man from Triton! Tell me, do all Tritonians have antennae like yours?"

"Yes," the alien said.

"And do they all have blue skin?"

"Yes," the alien replied.

"And do they all wear little caps on their heads?"

"No," the alien answered. "Not the goyim."

## FABRIC

1. When he manufactured the first corduroy pillows, Schlomo told reporters that he expected to make head lines. . . .

## FAIRY GODMOTHERS

1. After she was finished with Cinderella, the fairy godmother paid a visit on another poor young girl, Minuetta. Extremely flat-chested, the woman is convinced that her life would improve if only she had large breasts.

   "All right," the fairy godmother said. "How about we fix it so that every time a man says 'pardon' to you, your tits grow a bit."

   Delighted with the arrangement, Minuetta goes to market next day. Bumping into a woodcutter, she's delighted when he tips his hat, says, "I beg your pardon," and her breasts grow nearly an inch. Later, when a coachman accidentally splashes mud on her, he stops and says, "Pardon me." Her breasts grow again.

Smiling radiantly when she reaches the market, she goes to the vegetable stand and asks the Arab merchant for some bread. While he's handing it to her, he knocks a tub of jam on her dress.

"Oh dear," he bows and scrapes, "a thousand pardons!"

## FARMERS

See also DOGS 1, 9, INSANE ASYLUMS 3, SODOMY 1

1. "Say, Horace," one farmer asked the other, "you ever seen a egg plant?"

   "Certainly," replied the other.

   The first farmer shook his head. "Ya just *gotta* tell me how ya got far enough up the chicken's ass to look."

## FISH

See also FISHING

1. Q: What happens if you drink white wine with fish?
   A: The fish tend to get very abusive.

2. Q: How do you keep a killer fish behind bars?
   A: Strong lox.

3. After the fishing fleet had come and gone, the lonely fish looked around. Much to his horror, the empty seas confirmed what he had suspected—that he was, in fact, the sole survivor.

4. Q: How do baby fish swim?
   A: Roe after roe.

5. Q: Why did the restless parasite leave the eel?
   A: He felt he could travel faster on the pike.

## FISHING
See also FISH, IRANIANS 2

1. Jim and Pete went fishing. As soon as they got to the middle of the lake, Jim started reeling them in; Pete caught nothing.

   "It doesn't make any sense," Pete said. "My rod is better. I have more experience. But you're the one catching all the fish!"

   "That's because I have a *system*," Jim said. "Y'see, when I wake up, if my wife's sleeping on her left side, I fish the left side of the boat. If she's on her right side, I sit on the right side."

   "And what do you do if she's lying on her back?"

   Jim replied, "I don't go fishing."

2. Then there were the morons who went ice fishing. They caught a whopper, but drowned while frying it.

3. More practical was the beautiful young nurse who hated going fishing, but relished going down on the doc.

4. Willie and Hector were fishing off their row-boat, when Willie leaned too far over and his wallet fell into the water. Looking down into the lake, Willie reached for his wallet—just as a carp swooped over and snapped it up. As it swam away, another carp came over and grabbed it from the first. Then a third carp arrived and snatched the billfold.

   Amazed, Willie said to his friend, "Hector—you won't believe what I just saw."

   "What's that?"

   Willie replied, "Carp-to-carp walleting."

5. Then there were the Japanese fishers who presented a petition to the Soviet government, complaining that they were being harassed in international waters. The Soviets promised to mullet over. . . .

## FLAGS

1. Betsy Ross did more than make the first flag. When she finished, she asked people what they thought of it, thus also making the first flag-poll.

## FLATULENCE    See also DEFECATION, SKUNKS 1

1. Stepping into the elevator, Mr. Jeavons was alarmed by the odor which assailed him. Glowering at the only other occupant, a sweet old

lady, Jeavons asked, "Madam! Did you pass gas in here?"

"I most certainly did," replied the woman. "You don't think I smell like this normally, do you?"

## FOOD

See also CANDY, CHEFS, RESTAURANTS, JEWS 4, NUCLEAR ACCIDENTS 4, RUSSIANS 13, SALESPEOPLE 1, SEX 1, WORDPLAY 15

1. Q: What do you get from eating onions and beans?
   A: Tear gas.

2. Q: What did Kraft call the big food giveaway to promote its products?
   A: Chews for Cheeses. Naturally, the cry most frequently heard at the bash was "Gouda be praised!"

3. After a bitter marketing war, in which prices were continually being undercut, Birdseye and the Green Giant got together to settle their differences at a peas conference.

4. Q: How can you tell if pancakes are male or female?
   A: Female pancakes are stacked.

1. Losing by a wide margin, the fumble-plagued football team returned to the field after halftime. Going into the huddle, they suddenly dropped their pants and began jerking off.

   Horrified, the coach called the quarterback over. "What the hell are you guys *doing* out there?"

   The quarterback replied, "Coach, we're just doin' what you told us to."

   "What?"

   "Back in the locker room, you told us to go back out and pull ourselves together."

2. Fortunately for the masturbating squad, no one was arrested, since they were playing an exhibition game. . . .

3. "So," said the bartender to the football player, "I read in the paper you just got engaged."

   "No, it's off," the player said gloomily. "Just last night, she said she'd be true to the end."

   "I don't understand. What's wrong with that?"

   "What's wrong," said the player, "is that I'm the quarterback."

4. It had been an exhausting day of football, and the pigskin fanatic fell asleep in his chair. Rather

than wake him, his wife went to bed, expecting he'd join her later. Much to her surprise, however, when she woke up the next morning, he was still snoozing in front of the TV.

"Honey," she nudged him gently, "wake up. It's twenty to eight."

Starting, the man said, "Whose favor?"

5. Q: What's the difference between a quarterback and a virgin?
   A: One reels when the squad breaks through
   . . . .

6. Because he played for the Minnesota Vikings, old-time fullback Ron Bonelli was cremated on an open pyre. At the ceremony, however, a fan managed to get through security and began nagging current Vikings star Joe Pak with questions about the upcoming season.

   Finally growing tired of the young fan, Joe pushed him away. As he did so, however, Joe stumbled into the fire and perished along with the body of Ron Bonelli.

   As one newscaster later summed it up, for Joe it was a case of going from the prying fan into the pyre.

7. The star quarterback was informed that unless he could pass his math test, he wouldn't be allowed to play in the big game.

   The player worked hard all week, and when the professor handed him the exam booklet, the quarterback promptly stood, faded, and threw it squarely into the professor's arms.

8. When the quarterback finally understood what he was supposed to do with the test, he took it and flunked miserably. Desperate, the coach pleaded with the professor to allow him to take the test again.

"What for?" the instructor demanded. "The man is a complete idiot!" He threw open the book and pointed to the first problem. "Look at that! He wrote that ten plus ten is *thirty!*"

"C'mon," the coach implored, "give him a break. Christ, he was only off by five!"

9. The cheerleaders' new uniforms were the skimpiest ever seen in the NFL. Despite complaints from feminist groups, the designer insisted that the clothes would make the fans' root harder.

10. There was a great deal of sadness when quarterback Lech Stokowski graduated from the University of Warsaw. Not only did the football team lose a great player, but they no longer had ice water at the sidelines. Seems Lech took the recipe with him. . . .

11. Then there was the gay quarterback who was used only in emergencies. There was no one better when it came to engineering a come-from-behind victory.

12. It was a playoff game between the Jets and the Dolphins, and every seat in the stadium was occupied, save for one. Noticing it from the broadcast booth, the sportscaster went down to the seat during halftime.

"Do you happen to know why that seat is empty?" he asked a man sitting beside it.

"Yeah," he said around a mouthful of hotdog. "It's my wife's seat."

"Where is she?"

"She died," the man said.

Offering his sympathies, the sportscaster asked, "I'm surprised, though. Couldn't you find a friend to take it?"

The man shook his head. "Impossible. They're all at her funeral."

13. It was a tie game, fourth and goal from the two, and the quarterback was injured. Reluctantly the coach turned to his backup quarterback, a Pole named Cowsnofski.

"I can do it," the player said.

With no choice the coach put him in. At the snap Cowsnofski faded back and threw the pass of his life . . . nearly seventy yards.

## THE FOREIGN LEGION

1. Q: What do Foreign Legionnaires do on Saturday nights?
   A: Sit beneath palm trees and eat their dates.

1. "Madame Estelle," asked the man, "am I going to die?"

   "Die?" the woman replied. "That's the last thing you're going to do."

2. Looking at the man's palm, the gypsy said, "Sir, you are going to live to be ninety."

   The man replied, "But madam, I *am* ninety."

   The gypsy raised her hands in triumph. "What did I tell you?"


**THE FOURTH OF JULY**    *See also* BAKERS 1, SEX 4

1. Watching the other kids play with fireworks in a nearby pasture, the farm boy was frustrated being unable to take part. Pleading with one of the kids, the farm boy was allowed to buy a single firecracker. Not wanting to waste it on a measly little *pop*, he ran back to the farm, stuck it up the sheep's ass, and lit it.

   Then he stood back and smiled as it went off with a mighty *Ssssss . . . Boooom . . . Baaaaa-aaa!*

1. Every year at the state fair Paul entered the lottery for the brand-new truck—and lost. This year, he told his friend David, he wasn't going to bother to enter.

   "What kind of attitude is that?" David asked. He leaned closer and whispered, "What you need, pal, is *faith*. Look around and see if the good Lord sends you a message."

   Strolling around the fair, Paul grew more and more despondent as the drawing neared. Nothing struck him, no divine inspiration, no sign from God. Finally, while he was passing old Mrs. Kelleher's pie stand, he glanced over and saw the woman bending down. She wasn't wearing any panties, and suddenly her behind began to glow. Suddenly a finger of flame came from the skies and—without her even knowing it—used her ass as a tablet. The fiery finger etched a seven on each cheek.

   Thanking God, Paul rushed to the raffle booth and played the number 77.

   A few minutes later, the drawing was held. And once again Paul lost: the winning number was 707.


2. Stopping off at the local bar, farmer Meyers lay a sack on the floor and ordered a beer. His friend Attwood, a gambling man, ambled over.

   "Whatcha got in the bag, Meyers?"

"Got me some chickens to sell," the farmer replied.

"How about a little wager? If I can guess how many are in there, you give one to me."

Meyers stroked his chin. "Tell ya what. If you guess how many chickens I got, you can have them *both*."

3. Heading to Las Vegas, the vivacious divorcee met a handsome young man and went gambling with him. They stopped by the roulette wheel.

"What number do you think I should play?" she asked.

"Why not play your age?" he suggested.

Smiling, the woman put $100 on 34. The ball spun around, landing on 41; the woman promptly passed out.

4. Then there was the out-of-towner who on his very first day in Atlantic City lost all his money at the gaming tables. Since he wasn't ready to go home, he stood around and bet mentally. In no time flat, he lost his mind as well.

## GAMES                    *See also* CARDS, CHESS

1. Deciding that nothing would liven up the office party like charades, the president's secretary gathered everyone around and told them to act out emotions.

Everyone had a turn, and finally it was time for longtime mailroom employee Lincoln to do his charade. He promptly climbed up onto the buffet table, whipped out his penis, and lay on top of the large bowl of mousse.

There was a long, uneasy silence, after which the secretary asked, "A-and what emotion are you portraying, L-Lincoln."

He answered, "Lady, I'm just fuckin' dis custa'd."

2. Then there was the inventor of Scrabble, who used his life savings to market the game and hoped that people would sit down with it for a spell. . . .

## GENE SPLICING

1. Brilliant Dr. Penelope Curtis used gene splicing to produce a new strain of virus, Curtis Coccoloccocus. Unfortunately, she was exposed to the virus and became seriously ill, thereby proving that Curtis C *is* contagious.

## GENEALOGY

1. Visiting a genealogist, a man asked how much it would cost to have his family tree traced.

"It could cost thousands of dollars," said the woman.

"I see. Well, isn't there an easier way? A less expensive way?"

"Sure," she replied. "Run for president."

2. Regardless of the season, the family tree is the only one which can always be counted on to produce some nuts.

**GENITALS** *See also* SEX, ADAM AND EVE 1, CHEFS 3 COURTROOMS 9, DATING 6, 11, EVANGELISTS 1, GOLF 4, LANGUAGES 1, THE MUPPETS 1, PSYCHIATRISTS 9, SCHOOL 1, 8, X RAYS 1

1. An Italian, a Frenchman, and a Pole were discussing the reasons a man's penis had a head.

"That's simple," said the Italian. "It's there to give a man more pleasure."

*"Mais non,"* said the Frenchman. "The head is there to provide pleasure for the woman!"

"You're both nuts," said the Pole. "The head's there to keep your hand from slipping off."

2. Showering after a game of tennis, Lance happened to look over at Rod's genitals.

"Christ!" he exclaimed, "that's the biggest dick I've ever seen!"

Rod smiled. "It wasn't always that big. It grew because I rubbed it with butter every day."

Determined to improve his own endowment,

Lance went home to do likewise. The following week he and Rod played tennis again.

"How's it going with your . . . home improvements?" Rod asked.

"Terrible," Lance said. "I've been greasing my dick every day, but it keeps *shrinking!*"

"Really? Are you sure you're using enough butter?"

"Butter, hell. I'm allergic to dairy products, so I've been using Crisco."

Lance frowned. "Of course it's getting smaller. Crisco's *shortening!*"

3. On their wedding night the husband was so self-conscious about the smallness of his penis that before undressing, he snapped off the light.

Once he was in bed, he unzipped his pants and handed his member to his bride.

"That's thoughtful, darling," she cooed, "but we'll need the light if you want to write thank-you notes."

4. Q: What do you call a vagina that talks back to you?
   A: An answering cervix.

5. Erik thought he'd heard the ultimate in braggadocio when he was walking home from a bar with his friends Hal and Jack. They'd been arguing about whose penis was longer, and when they'd stopped on a bridge to urinate, Hal had said, "Hey, this water's cold!"

Jack had replied, "And it's deep, too."

However, nothing could top the flea who was floating toward them on his back and yelling, "Raise the drawbridge! Raise the drawbridge!"

6. While making love together for the first time, Teddy was furious when his girlfriend suddenly stopped and lay back.

   "What's wrong?" he demanded.

   "Forgive me," she said, "but it's your organ. It just isn't big enough."

   "Forgive *me*," George replied, "but it wasn't meant to be played in a cathedral!"

7. While a hunky patient was having a body cast removed, one of the nurses at the hospital happened to notice that he had the word "Little" tattooed on the shaft of his penis.

   Curious, she mentioned this to a coworker, then arranged to go out on a date with the patient. The next morning she came to work with a huge smile on her face.

   "I don't understand it," the coworker said. "Why on earth would you want to go out with a man who had the word 'Little' on his penis."

   "Because," she said. "when I stroked it, I found out that it said, 'Little Anthony's Pizza —we deliver twenty-four hours a day, every day of the year.' "

8. Then there was the man so over-endowed, he had a fiveskin.

9. While he was at the booksellers' convention, Dinsdale met an achingly attractive editor, whom he promptly asked for a date. She accepted, and before long they both ended up back in Dinsdale's hotel room. Unfortunately, no matter what the editor did, no matter how she coaxed his member, Dinsdale was unable to raise an erection.

Upon returning home the following night, he greeted his wife and took a shower. When he stepped out, she was lying in bed, all three hundred pounds of her stuffed into a tattered nightgown, her hair in curlers, a mudpack on her face, watching television.

Suddenly he found himself possessed by a spectacular erection. Looking down at his attentive member, Dinsdale screamed, "Why you backward, confused thing! No *wonder* they call you a prick!"

10. Walking up to the counter in the record store, the luscious young lady asked the man, "Do you have U2's latest?"

"What I got for you," the man said, leaning closer, "is an eight-inch schlong."

Puzzled, the girl asked, "Is that a record?"

"No," the clerk said, "but it's far better than average."

11. Bubba worked in the mailroom of a large corporation. He was a husky man, but also a lazy one; more often than not, toward the end of the

day he could be found fast asleep behind the mail carts.

One day young Ms. Smith came back with her mail. Finding Bubba asleep, she allowed curiosity to get the best of her. Never having seen a black man's member, she quietly unzipped his pants and took it out. Amazed by its size, she fondled it for a moment, then decided she had to have it when Bubba was awake. Lacking a pen or paper, she simply took the blue ribbon from her hair and tied it to the organ, hoping he'd get the message.

A few minutes after Ms. Smith left, Bubba awoke. Looking down at his penis, he noticed the adornment and smiled.

"Shit," he said, "I don't know what we been up to, but I'll be damned if we didn't take first place!"

12. Then there was a man who complained to his psychiatrist that he had an inferiority complex about the diminutive size of his penis.

Smiling, the shrink said, "Oh, I wouldn't let a little thing like that trouble you!"

**GERMS** See also GENE SPLICING

1. As was their habit, Marsha and Mel made love every night precisely at 9:20. Even when Marsha came down with the flu, they didn't break their tradition; the doctor gave her an

antibiotic which killed all but three of the germs.

Hiding from the medicine, one germ said, "Lissen, I'm gonna go hide in her eyelashes. The antibiotics won't think to look for me there."

"Me?" said the second. "I'm headin' for her ear. I'll bury myself in wax and they'll never find me."

The third virus shook its head. "You go where you want, fellas, but when that ol' 9:20 pulls out, your's truly's gonna be on it!"

## GHOSTS

1. The parapsychologist had devoted her life to one goal: obtaining photographic proof of the existence of ghosts. Learning of a house which was haunted by a very active and very visible poltergeist, she hurried over.

It was night, and the ghost had tugged out all of the fuses, leaving the home in pitch blackness. Making her way slowly, the woman spied a glowing ball of ectoplasm at the top of a staircase. Unable to check the setting on her camera, she took a chance and shot the entire roll on one setting. Not only didn't the ghost move the entire time, but it actually posed and made faces at her each time the flash-cubes flared.

Unfortunately, when she had the roll developed, the pictures were completely under-exposed. As she morosely explained it to a colleague, "The spirit was willing, but the flash was weak."

2. After spending all their money on home improvements, the Amityville couple had nothing left to pay their exorcist. Needless to say, their house was promptly repossessed.

## GIRL SCOUTS

1. Snuggling into her scout uniform, the young girl paused to admire her blossoming form in the mirror.

   "Mama, look!" she said. "I've got titties! Big titties!"

   The woman said, "Now, Ruth, we don't call them that!"

   "Then what should I call them?" the girl asked.

   Thinking quickly, the woman said, "Brownie points."

## GOATS

1. The two goats wandered into the junkyard and had a field day. One of them spent a particularly long time bent over a spool of film.

When he was finished, the other goat came over. "So, did you enjoy the film?"

The goat replied, "To tell you the truth, I liked the book better."

GOD
See also CLERGY, EVANGELISTS, HEAVEN, JESUS CHRIST, CASTRO 2, GAMBLING 1, GOLF 2

1. Looking unusually pale, the pope called together all of his cardinals. "My devoted flock," he said in a voice that was barely above a whisper, "I have good news, I have bad news, and I have terrible news. The good news is that I've spoken with God. The bad news is that it's a *she*."

   "She?" cried one of the cardinals.

   "Yes," said the pope.

   "After all we've said about abortion and women," muttered another cardinal, "what could be worse than that?"

   The pope replied, "She was calling from Salt Lake City."

2. Lying on his deathbed in the small Southern hospital, an old black preacher had a Bible on his chest, his hands folded atop it.

   "Almighty God," he said, "I been your faithful servant all my life. This one time, I beg you to answer just one question so I can tell the rest of the flock. Lord God, are you black or are you white?"

Suddenly the room darkened, a ball of light appeared near the ceiling, and a voice rumbled, "I am what I am."

The old man's face wrinkled. "Please, Lord, that's no answer. I *need to know!*"

The voice boomed again, "Dummy! If I were black, I would have said unto Moses and now unto you, 'I be what I be.' "

3. Straight out of college and not terribly sharp, young Burton nonetheless lands a choice assignment: to interview both the president of the United States and the prime minister of Israel.

Heading to the White House, Burton is ushered into the Oval Office. Looking at the chief executive's desk, he asks what each of the telephones is for.

"This one," says the president, "is a direct line to the chairman of the Soviet Union. The one next to it is a direct line to the prime minister of Israel. And the one next to that is a direct line to God."

"God!" the reporter gasps, scribbling furiously, "Gee, how much does it cost to call God?"

"Oh, about ten thousand dollars a minute," says the president.

Completing the interview, Burton hops onto a plane and flies to Tel Aviv. After being introduced to the prime minister, they sit down at his desk. Burton asks what all of the phones are for.

"With this one," he says, "I can talk directly to the president of the United States. And with this one, I can telephone the president of Egypt."

"And the one next to it?" Burton asks.

"It's a special line," the Prime Minister says. "With it, I can talk directly to God."

"And how much does it cost *you*," Burton asks.

"A quarter."

"A quarter? But the president told me it costs *him* ten thousand dollars!"

"That's true," the prime minister replies. "But from here, it's a local call."

4. Whipping up his best oratory, the Republican candidate for president campaigned deep in the heart of the Democratic city. At the end of a fiery speech he said, "To those of you who vote Democratic solely from tradition, I say— change! To those who refuse to consider the candidate, I say—it pains me to think that you would vote Democratic even if God Himself ran as a Republican!"

Said a voice from the crowd: "Why would He bother to change parties?"

**GOLF** *See also* BLACKS 2

1. After his youthful partner comes in to ask the doctor for his opinion on a diagnosis, the elder physician says, "Nerves and vomiting, eh?"

"That's right. But there are no physical causes that I can find."

"Don't worry, I've seen this before," the doctor says. "Ask the patient if he plays golf. If he says no, tell him to start. If he says yes, tell him to stop."

2. Three men are playing golf—Moses, Jesus, and an elderly gentleman. Moses is the first to tee off and, hitting the ball, he sends it smack into a lake. Undaunted, he saunters over, raises his hands, parts the water, and hits the ball onto the green.

Next up is Jesus, who also lobs the ball into the water. Strolling out to the middle of the lake, he bends down and also knocks the ball onto the green.

Finally it's the old man's turn. He hits the ball, which also heads for the water. However, a turtle happens to surface then, and the ball ricochets off its shell, is caught by a pelican which happens to be passing by, falls from its mouth, strikes a tree, and rolls down a limb where a squirrel grabs it. The furry creature carries it to the cup and drops it in.

Flushing with anger, Jesus turns and says, "Impressive, dad, but are you here to screw around or play golf?"

3. Visiting New York from the Midwest, the ad exec's client said that what he really enjoyed

was swinging nightclubs. So the exec took him to an illuminated golf course. . . .

4. Then there was the country club president who was dismissed following a competition between the women of all the local golf courses. Seems he presented the winner with a trophy engraved, "Intercourse champion of the county."

5. The young man had just teed up on the first hole, and was getting ready to drive when a woman in a wedding dress came running toward him. She grabbed his arm and began shouting as she pulled him toward the parking lot.

"For God's sake," the man screamed back, "I said only if it rains!"

6. Getting ready to go to the golf club with his grandfather, the young boy was looking around the trunk of the new BMW.

"What're these?" he asked, pulling a small sack from the golf bag after his grandfather had loaded his clubs.

"Those are tees," the old man said. "You put your balls in them when you drive."

"Golly," the boy said, "those BMW people think of everything, don't they?"

## GRAMMAR

1. "Tell me," the teacher asked her students, "do you know what the word 'can't' is short for?"

   "Yes," said little Bette. "It's short for 'cannot.' "

   "Very good. And what about 'don't '?"

   Little Marty's hand shot up. "That," he said with authority, "is short for 'doughnut.' "

## GRANDPARENTS

1. Young Jason was sleeping on the sofa with his grandfather so that he and the old man could get up early the next morning and go fishing.

   During the middle of the night the elderly gentleman started awake. "Jason! Run and get your grandmother quick, and then stay in the bedroom."

   Sighing, Jason said, "Cool it, Grampa. That's *my* dick you're holding."

## GYNECOLOGISTS      *See also* DOCTORS, PREGNANCY 3

1. He was a gynecologist with a sense of humor: whenever he made the rounds at the old age home, he introduced himself as a spreader of old wives' tails.

2. Then there was the blind gynecologist who made his living by reading lips.

## THE HANDICAPPED

*See also* THE BLIND, SPEECH IMPEDIMENTS, MASTURBATION 5, SKUNKS 1

1. Armless Dan walked into the bar and ordered a beer. "Would you mind pouring it?" he asked the bartender. "It's not easy for me."

   The bartender obliged.

   "Thanks," said Dan. "Now would you mind holding the stein for me? It'll save me a lot of trouble."

   Once again the bartender was happy to help.

   "The money," Dan said. "It's in my vest pocket. If you wouldn't mind taking it out—"

   The bartender didn't mind at all.

   When he was finished, Dan looked around. "One more thing. Where's the rest room?"

   "In the back," the bartender said, pointing. "You go through that door—alone."

2. Walking into the lingerie store, the hard-of-hearing customer says to the clerk, "I'd like to buy a pair of stockings for my wife."

   The clerk says, "Sheer?"

   And the man replies, "No. She's in another store."

3. It was a day long anticipated by the dashing Prince Herbert: he was finally to meet the

princess to whom he had been betrothed as a babe.

With much pomp and fanfare the princess's entourage entered the throne room, after which her highness herself was shown to the prince. When she curtsied, he gasped: to his horror, the woman was monstrously obese, nearly bald, had a glass eye which rolled grotesquely around its socket, and when she smiled, Herbert saw just one tooth in her mouth.

Leaning over to the king, Prince Herbert said into his ear, "Father! How could you *do* this to me! The princess is a . . . a monster!"

"No need to whisper, son," the king bellowed. "She's deaf, too."

## HATS
See also CLOTHING, BRASSIERES 2, CRIME 1, LOGIC 2, MURDER 2, PSYCHIATRISTS 1

1. Incredible as it may seem, no one recognized the Shriner after he had his fez lifted.

## HEALTH

1. Spotting a shrunken, elderly man sitting contentedly at a table in the singles' bar, sexy, jaded Yvette slinked over.

"Say," she said, "it's unusual to see a man like you in here. You look as if you don't have a worry in the world."

"I don't," he admitted.

She leaned close to his ear and said longingly, "Tell me. What's the secret of your happiness?"

"Well," he said, "to start with, I chain smoke. I also drink a fifth of scotch in the morning, and another in the evening. I don't exercise, and I eat whatever the hell I please."

"That's incredible," she said. "And how old are you?"

He answered, "Twenty."

**HEAVEN** *See also* GOD, CELEBRITIES 4,
INFIDELITY 1, THE IRISH 2, MUSSOLINI 5,
PREJUDICE 3, VENEREAL DISEASES 4

1. Due to an error in bookkeeping, the devout Sister Elizabeth was sent to hell instead of heaven. Allowed the customary one phone call, she rang St. Peter.

"You must transfer me out of here!" she wailed. "There's an orgy scheduled for this evening!"

St. Peter assured her he'd do what he could. However, his backlog of work was extraordinary, and he forgot about Sister Elizabeth until the following morning, when he found a message on his answering machine: "Pete," it said, "this is Liz. Forget about the transfer."

2. After a tragic fire in a Catholic school, three young ladies arrived in heaven. They were

met by St. Peter, who told them that all each of them had to do to be admitted beyond the pearly gates was to answer a question about the Bible.

The first young woman faced St. Peter. "What," he asked, "was the name of the first man?"

"Adam," she answered, and was admitted.

The second young woman approached St. Peter. "What," he asked, "was the name of the first woman?"

"Eve," she said, and the gates swung wide for her.

The third young woman approached St. Peter. "What," he asked, "was the first thing Eve said to Adam?"

The young woman wrung her hands. "Gee, sir, that's hard."

St. Peter stepped aside and admitted her.

3. As sometimes happens, the bookkeepers in heaven were backlogged and couldn't record everyone who's in line at the pearly gates. Thus, St. Peter went to the two men at the back of the line and told them he's sending them back to earth for a month.

"Because you're doing us a favor," St. Peter said, "I'm going to allow you to return as anything you wish."

"Gee," said the first man, "I've always wanted to be a condor soaring majestically through the skies of California."

With a wave of his hand St. Peter granted the man his wish.

Stroking his chin, the second man said, "Y'know, I've always wanted to be a stud in New York."

With a wave of his hand St. Peter also granted the second man his wish.

A month passed, and after the backlog had been cleared up, St. Peter summoned a pair of angels. "It's time to go and get the men I returned to earth."

"How will we recognize them?" one angel asked.

"Well," St. Peter replied, "the first one won't be a problem. There aren't many condors left in California. As for the second, that's a problem. There's a lot of new construction going on in Manhattan. . . ."

4. After countless centuries the wall between heaven and hell began to crack from the extreme heat on the underside. Slipping through the fissure, St. Peter confronted Satan.

"You know, Lucifer, for the past thirty centuries, we've been doing the repairs whenever there's a break in the wall. God feels it's time you did *your* fair share."

Twirling his tail, Satan barked, "Forget it! My demons are too busy to bother with a stinking wall."

Indignant, St. Peter said, "In that case, I'm afraid we have no recourse but to sue you."

"Oh?" grinned the Devil. "And where do you intend to find a lawyer?"

## HISTORY See also RUSSIANS 10, THANKSGIVING 2

1. Wanting to know whether Cleopatra had been faithful to him, the noble Mark Anthony came right out and asked—and was surprised when the bright young queen answered by invoking another man's name. She said, simply "Omar Khayyam."

2. The student from Massachusetts was touring San Antonio when he stopped and tugged a Texan's sleeve.

"Excuse me, sir," said the New Englander, "but what building is that?"

"Building?" blurted the Texan. "Why son, that's the Alamo! That's where just over a hundred Texans held off five thousand crack Mexican troops."

"I see," said the Northerner. "And the statue over there. Who's that?"

"Why, that's John Reid, the Texas Ranger who tracked down over one hundred killers, rustlers, injuns, and Mexicans single-handed." Taking in both shrines with a sweep of his hand, the Texan said, "Mighty impressive, eh, boy?"

The student shrugged. "I don't know. We Massachusettsites have a hero too. Paul Revere."

"Revere?!" the Texan exclaimed. "Y'mean, that wimp who had to ride for help?"

3. It was an oral exam in ancient history, and the teacher knew that R. J. hadn't studied. Thus she called on him first.

    "R. J.," she said, "I would like you to name two sports of Ancient Rome."

    Knitting his brow, he said, "Nero and Claudius?"

4. Q: What did Betsy Ross take to determine what the new U.S. banner should look like?
   A: A flag poll.

5. While collecting tickets on a train, conductor Rufus struck up a conversation with a passenger, who happened to be a rare-book dealer.

    "Y'know," Rufus said, "it's fittin' that I should meet you. Last week someone left a real old book on the train. I threw it out. It was a Bible, I think. Had a funny name on it—Gluten or Gootin, somethin' like that."

    The bookseller paled. "Dear Lord. Don't tell me the name was *Gutenberg*."

    "Yeah, that was it! Gutenberg."

    The book dealer buried his face in his hands. "Sweet Jesus. Do you have any idea how much that book was worth?"

    "Not very much, I'll bet," Rufus said confidently. "Someone by the name of Martin Luther wrote all over the damn thing."

1. Lying down on the psychiatrists's couch, the young man said to the doctor, "I wanted to see you because I think I'm gay."

   "Oh?" said the doctor. "And what makes you think that?"

   "Well, my grandfather was gay, and so was my father."

   "That doesn't mean you're gay," said the psychiatrist. "We don't believe that homosexuality is hereditary."

   "Maybe not, but my two brothers are also gay."

   "Really?" said the doctor, intrigued.

   "That's right. And so are my two uncles and my cousin."

   "That *is* uncanny," said the psychiatrist, his interest greatly piqued. "Tell me—isn't there anyone in your family who has sex with women?"

   "Yes, sir," the young man said. "My sister."

2. Q: How can you tell if a weightlifter is gay?
   A: He's the one who's pumping Myron. . . .

3. Q: What's a popular card game in gay circles?
   A: Poker—with no straights allowed, and queens wild.

4. "Hey, Marvin!" the gay man called to his lover, "has the mailman come yet?"

   "No," Marvin yelled back, "but he's starting to moan."

5. After examining the scene of the murder, the inspector said to his colleague, "Arrest this man's lover."

   "You mean, Bruce? But I thought this was a suicide."

   "No," said the inspector. "Homocide."

6. Then there were the two very contented Irish gays, Henry Fitzpatrick and Patrick Fitzhenry.

7. Then there was the gay Arab who went around with tongue in sheik.

8. Q: What do you call Bloomingdale's when all the gay employees are home sick?
   A: Closed.

9. Q: What's the difference between the fruits in California and Florida?
   A: In Florida, *you* pick the fruits. . . .

10. And, of course, the difference between gays in the North and in the South is that in the South, they call them "homosex y'alls."

11. And let's not forget the gay nail who gave up a life of luxury in the wall in order to lay in the road and blow tires.

12. . . . or the gay who was drummed off the baseball team for dropping every fly that came his way.

13. Which wasn't as bad as the lady tennis star who alarmed her competitors when she came to the tournament and boldly announced that she'd lick everyone who played her. . . .

14. . . . or the male hairdresser whose colleagues called him a pervert for going out with women . . . .

15. Finally there's the bisexual gopher, who digs everybody's hole.

**HONEYMOONS**                    *See also* MARRIAGE,
                                  SEX, GENITALS 3

1. The morning after their wedding night, a man woke up to find his innocent young bride sobbing.

   "What's wrong?" he asked, putting his arm around her.

   "It's last night . . ." she wept.

   "Last night? Did I hurt you? Didn't you enjoy it?"

   "Oh, it was wonderful," she said, then pointed to his bare crotch. "But—look! After just one night we used it all up!"

2. Robert wanted many things in a wife, but above all he wanted one who was a virgin. Falling madly in love with Rebecca, he decided to test her.

At a drive-in one night, he leaned over and said, "Would you like to see my pee-pee?"

As he unzipped his fly, Rebecca covered her eyes. "No! No! Please put it back!"

Thrilled, he deemed Rebecca worthy of being his bride, and immediately proposed to her. On their wedding night he was keenly anticipating the delight of introducing his bride to sex.

When she came to bed, he unzipped his fly and took out his member.

Rebecca smiled. "Ooooh . . . what a nice pee-pee."

Robert stroked her hair. "My dear, the first thing you must learn is that it really isn't called a pee-pee. It's called a cock."

"No," she said, studying it, "that's a pee-pee. A cock is long, fat, and black."

3. Following a session of lovemaking, the new Mrs. Dexter suddenly turned and socked her husband in the belly.

"What's that for?" he demanded.

"That's for being a lousy lover," she complained.

After a moment Mr. Dexter turned and smacked his bride in the ass.

"What's *that* for?" she asked.

He replied, "Knowing the difference."

4. Because his fiancée Patti was a virgin and frightened of sex, Craig wanted to do everything he could to make their wedding night memorable. He even took Patti's mother aside and suggested that she make her a negligee, something to make her feel especially sexy.

The woman agreed. Buying the pinkest fabric she could find, she made a skimpy garment and gave it to Craig, who put it in a small box.

Finally the big night arrived. Patti was wearing a bathrobe buttoned to the neck. Realizing that it would be best not to alarm her with the sight of his member, Craig said softly to his new bride, "I'm going into the bathroom to undress. Whatever you do, don't look at me. We'll save that for later." Then, kissing her, he handed Patti the box. "In the meantime I want you to put this on. For me."

Craig left and, her heart thumping, Patti slowly undid the wrapping. Her fingers trembling, she lifted the lid. Reaching in, she took out the garment and held it up. Her jaw dropped.

"My God!" she exclaimed. "What on earth is this pink, wrinkled little thing?"

From the bathroom Craig yelled, "Darn it, hon, I *told* you not to look!"

5. In the week before his marriage David sowed the last of his wild oats with all the girls he'd ever dated. At the end of that time his penis was literally twisted and broken.

David begged his doctor to help him, but

the best the physician could do was create a makeshift splint, taping the worn member between four thin slats.

On his wedding night David crawled into bed with his new bride, wondering what he'd tell her about his ravaged organ.

The woman spread her legs. "Look, honey," she said. "Never been touched by a man."

Smiling, David undid his pajama pants. "Look, honey," he said. "Still in its original crate!"

**HORSE RACES**　　　*See also* GAMBLING, HORSES, JOURNALISM 1

1. After leaving the racetrack Jake bumped into his old friend Peter on the bus.

"Say," Peter said, "how's it going?"

"Going? You wanna hear one of the most amazing things that ever happened? Tell me—what's today's date?"

"July seventh."

"Right. The seventh day of the seventh month. I got to the track at seven minutes past seven. My son is seven years old today, and we live at number seven Seventh Avenue."

"Let me guess," Peter interrupted. "You put everything you had on the seventh horse in the seventh race."

"Right."

"And he won!?"

Peter sighed. "No. He came in seventh."

1. The Atlanta team was in the cellar of their division, and the manager was afraid of losing his job. Thus, when a horse sauntered into the stadium during practice one afternoon and said he could hit a baseball a quarter mile, the manager actually handed him a bat and told him to prove it.

   Walking over to the plate, the horse crouched on its hind legs, picked up the bat, and promptly sent the first pitch soaring over the fence, past the parking lot, and into the next county. The second pitch, a screwball, followed the first. The third pitch, a fast ball, actually smoked as it sailed through the sky.

   The manager signed the horse without further ado, and put him at fourth in the batting order. No one could have been happier when, with bases loaded, the animal headed for the plate. He watched the pitch—a slider—swung, and sent it rocketing into the stratosphere.

   But he just stood there.

   Frantic, the manger screamed, "Run, goddamit! *Run!*"

   Disgusted, the horse looked back. "Putz! If I could run, I'd still be at Belmont!"

## HOSPITALITY

1. A remnant of the old South, Colonel Lee was strolling through his mansion when he saw his daughter and her beau on the marble floor of the foyer, making mad love.

    "Scahlett!" the Colonel roared, "where *are* yo' mannuhs? You arch yo' back this *instant* and lift that gen'man's testicles off the cold flo'!"

## HUCKSTERS

1. By far the biggest attraction at the country fair was Dr. Mirakle's tent. In it the young-looking man who claimed to be two hundred years old was selling an elixir which was guaranteed to keep people eternally youthful.

    "I don't believe it," a grumpy old man said to the huckster's aide, a beautiful young woman. "Tell me the truth, miss. Is that guy really as old as he says?"

    The woman leaned over and whispered, "To tell you the truth, sir, I have my doubts. But then, I only met him in 1837."

1. As luck would have it, the very first time the moron went hunting, he was killed by his prey. He was following some tracks when all of a sudden the train came along and hit him.

2. Then there was the other moron who went hunting. On his way to the hunting grounds he came across a sign which read, "BEAR LEFT," so he turned the car around and went home.

3. Two other morons went hunting in the woods. Before long, however, they realized they had no idea how to get back to civilization.

   "Not to worry," one of them said. "When you're lost, all you have to do is fire three shots in the air."

   They did so and waited; an hour later they did it again, and still no one came. Finally they tried a third time.

   "This better work," one man said to the other. "These're our last arrows."

4. Then there was still another moron who was out hunting when he spied a beautiful young woman sunbathing, nude, in a clearing. Walking over, he said, "Pardon me, ma'am, but are you game?"

   Looking the hunky fellow up and down, she replied, "Sure."

   So he shot her.

5. Finally, there was the Polish big game hunter who gave up the profession after just a week. He got tired of lugging around the decoys.


## IMMIGRANTS

1. A few days after entering the U.S., Herman M'tube was summoned to the immigration bureau.

   "Mr. M'tube," said the officer, "I'm sorry to say we're going to have to deport you."

   "But why?" the African asked.

   "Because you lied on your immigration papers. It asked if you have any relatives abroad, and you said no. Yet we've learned that you have a brother in South Africa."

   "That is true, sir," said M'tube. "But he is at home. It is I who am abroad."


2. It was the immigrant's first time at a baseball game. His friend cheered wildly each time a batter came to the plate, and after a while the immigrant cheered as well.

   After Vinnie DiFate had had his turn at bat, the immigrant shouted, "Run, Vinnie, run!"

   "No," his friend said, "Vinnie has four balls, so he walks."

   Eyes wide, the immigrant yelled, "Walk tall, Vinnie! Walk tall!"

1. Seventy-year-old Mr. Berkowitz went to see his doctor.

   "Morty," he said, "I need something which will enable me to get an erection. What can you do?"

   The doctor gave the man a shot of a potency drug, but only charged him $50 for the office visit.

   A few days later, thrilled with the results, Mr. Berkowitz returned for a second injection. Only this time, before leaving, he gave the doctor a crisp $100 bill.

   "But the bill is only $50."

   "I know," he winked. "The other $50 is from my wife."

## *INCEST*     *See also* SEX

1. Q: What's a virgin in the deep South?
   A: A girl who can outrun her brothers.

## *INDIANS*

1. While traveling through Arizona, Mr. Goldstein stopped at an impoverished Indian reservation. There he saw a young man and his father making trinkets for tourists.

"Excuse me," Mr. Goldstein said to the old man, "but don't you think your boy would be better off if he got an education?"

"He would," the Indian agreed, "but I can't afford one."

"Don't worry," Mr. Goldstein said. "I have a factory in Brooklyn. He can work there and go to school at night."

The old man thought for a minute. "Our culture is very important to us, but so is education. Thank you, sir. He will go with you."

Two years passed, and, finally the young Indian returned to the reservation. As he stepped from the bus, he was still wearing the clothing he had had on when he left, still carried himself with the pride of a Native American.

"My son," the old Indian embraced him, "I'm glad to see that the city did not change you."

"No, father," the youth said. "Vonce an Indian, alvays an Indian."

2. Q: What did the Indian say when the mushroom cloud rose above the desert.
   A: "There's no need to yell!"

3. Then, of course, there was the witty Indian, who, after the famous battle, opined that General Custer definitely blew the Little Big Horn.

4. Q: In *1,001 Great Jokes*, we asked: What did the Indian say when he'd bagged a doe without eyes? His response: "I have

no eye deer." Out hunting again, the Indian kills a deer with no eyes *or* legs. What does he have?

A: "Still no eye deer."

Q: Going out a third time, he shoots a deer with no eyes, legs, or genitals. What does he have now?

A: "Still no fucking eye deer."

5. Q: What rock music station do they listen to on reservations?

A: MTP.


**INDUSTRY**     *See also* BUSINESS, CHEWING GUM 1


1. Much to his surprise, the foreman of a match factory was told that he was going to be awarded the coveted Congressional Medal of Honor.

"Thank you," he said to the government official, "but why have I been singled out for this honor?"

"Because you're a typical American worker who helped to avert a disaster."

"I did?"

"Yes. Last week a terrorist tried to start a fire at a nuclear power plant in Pennsylvania. He didn't succeed."

"I still don't understand," said the foreman.

The official explained, "The matches failed to light."

2. Coming downstairs to inspect the shipments of imported crystal vases leaving the plant, the foreman approached his new packer. He put his arm around the man's shoulder.

"Well, Olshevski, I see you did what I asked. Stamped the top of each box, 'THIS SIDE UP, HANDLE WITH CARE.'"

"Yes sir," the worker replied. "And just to make sure, I stamped it on the bottom, too."

## INFIDELITY

See also SEX, BASEBALL 5, CONFESSION 2, DOCTORS 4, FOOTBALL 3, GENITALS 9, MORONS 1 MURDER 1, SEX 21

1. A man arrived at his apartment to find his wife lying naked in bed, the sheets a mess, and the smell of pipe tobacco in the air.

Running to the window, he spotted a man with a pipe walking down the street. Grabbing a nearby grandfather clock, he dragged it to the window and pushed it out. It landed on the man's head and crushed him. However, the exertion took its toll on the irate husband and, suffering a heart attack, he died.

When he opened his eyes, he found himself standing before St. Peter. Beside him were two men, one of whom was smoking a pipe.

"Well," said St. Peter, "before I can admit you, I must know how each of you died."

The man with the pipe said, "Sir, I was

simply walking down the street, bothering no one, when I was struck by a grandfather clock."

The husband said, "Sir, I died from the strain of lifting the grandfather clock."

The third man says, "Well, sir, I was hiding inside this grandfather clock. . . ."

2. Juan came to visit his friend Leroy in the hospital. He was shocked at his friend's condition: his right arm and both legs were in casts, there was a bandage around his head and across his nose, both eyes were black, and even his dick was in a sling.

"Christ," Juan said, "what happened to you?"

"Well," Leroy said through his missing teeth, "you know Mrs. Huxtable?"

"The cute babe down the street?"

"That's the one. Well, I was in mid-stroke with her, when her goddamn construction worker husband came home early."

Juan looked his friend up and down. "It's bad, buddy, but you know—it could've been worse."

"Really? How?"

Juan said, "If he'd come home an hour earlier, he'd've beat the shit out of *me*."

3. Then there was a survey in which nearly one-third of the husbands responded that they talk to their wives after sex—but only if there were a telephone handy.

4. "It's terrible," Kevin said to his friend. "My wife and my friend Bill just hopped in my car and drove off for parts unknown."

"That *is* terrible," replied the friend. "You just bought that car, didn't you?"

5. "What would you say if I told you I was having an affair with your best friend?" Mrs. Stewart asked her husband.

Mr. Stewart replied, "I'd say you were a dyke."

6. Sitting at the bar, glum Roger told the barkeeper that he was drinking to forget the heartbreak of his broken engagement.

"Yeah," said Roger, "would you marry someone who didn't know the meaning of the word faithful, and who was flip and even vicious when the subject of fidelity came up?"

"No way in hell," the bartender said.

"Well," said Roger, "neither would my fiancée."

7. A construction worker, Ramsey decided to work late one Friday night in order to earn overtime. However, he was at a remote site, and had no way of letting his wife know he'd be late. His foreman offered to stop by on his way home and tell her.

When he arrived, Ramsey's wife caused his eyes to bulge—among other things.

"I hope you don't take this wrong," he said,

"but you're the most fetching thing I've ever seen!"

The woman blushed.

"Y'know," he said, "Ramsey's said you've been having money problems. Why don't you help him out? I'll give you one hundred dollars for an hour in bed."

The woman recoiled. "Sir! I would never do that to my husband."

"What about for two hundred dollars? Think about it. He doesn't have to know, and you'll have him home more often."

The woman's resistance seemed to soften.

"Three hundred?" the foreman said.

"Well," said the woman, "as long as he never finds out."

With that, she led the man to the bedroom. Later that night Ramsey came home exhausted. After kissing his wife, he asked, "Did my boss come by and tell you I was working overtime?"

"Yes he did," she said.

"Good. And did he also give you my pay?"

8. The siren nearly blew the head off his beer. Looking out the window of the bar moments later, Delaney saw a fire engine go racing by.

"Well," he said to the bartender, "I'm off."

"Wait a minute. I didn't know you were a volunteer fireman!"

"I'm not," said Delaney, finishing his beer, "but my girlfriend's husband *is*."

9. After returning from a lengthy business trip, Ronald was chatting over the fence with his neighbor Phil.

"Say," Phil said, "your eyes look really red. Is everything all right?"

Ronald leaned closer. "Can you keep a secret, pal?" Phil said he could, and Ronald said, "It happened the very first night I was in San Juan. I met a woman in the hotel lounge, a beautiful gal. We had a few drinks, one thing led to another, and pretty soon we were back in her room. The next morning I woke up and found her crying in the bathroom. She said that she was married, and was ashamed about what we did.

"As soon as I heard that, I started feeling guilty myself about Lisa and the kids, and I began crying too."

"But, Ron," Phil said, "you left two weeks ago! Why are your eyes bloodshot today?"

"Christ," Ronald said, "you can't cry every damn morning for two weeks without making them red!"

10. Meanwhile, Ronald had no reason to feel guilty. Going to a bar one night, Lisa told the bartender, "It's awful. My husband is constantly away on business trips." She looked the young man straight in the eye. "Tell me. What would you do in my place?"

After work he showed her.

11. Pleased with the results of the evening courses he was taking at a local college, Jacinto said to his friend Donato, "Say, I bet you can't tell me who Ernest Hemingway is!" Donato admitted he could not, and Jacinto said, "He was a famous American author. Now, I bet you can't tell me who Percival Lowell is." Donato acknowledged that once again he was at a disadvantage. "He was a famous American astronomer," Jacinto replied.

Donato nodded. "Since you're so smart, my friend, can you tell me who Bubba Nelson is?"

Jacinto scratched his head. "Sorry, I never heard of him."

Donato grinned. "He's the famous American electrician who comes to see your wife when you're at school."

12. Then there was the sage who pointed out that infants don't have nearly as much fun in infancy as adults have in adultery.

## INSANE ASYLUMS     See also PSYCHIATRISTS, ART 2

1. After ten years of incarceration in an insane asylum, the remarkable Ralph Dibney seemed to have made a remarkable recovery.

"While you were here," the doctor said, "you actually acquired a doctorate in chemistry. If I recommend that you be released, what do you plan to do?"

"I plan to go to work doing R&D for a major corporation."

"Good . . . and if you can't get a job?"

"Then I'll see if I can get a grant and open my own lab."

"Very sound," the doctor agreed. "And if those options fail?"

"Well," Dibney shrugged, "I can always get a job as a doorbell."

2. Escaping from the men's section of the insane asylum, the retardate made his way into the women's block. There he noticed a woman with practically no clothes. He took her in his arms.

Nine months later, he escaped again and returned to her room. Only this time she had a little moron.

3. It was Loomis's day to walk about the grounds of the asylum. Pausing by the fence, he looked into the fields of the farmer next door.

"Hey," he yelled, "what the heck're you doing?"

"Spreading fertilizer on the strawberries," the farmer replied.

Shaking his head, Loomis says, "Fella, you oughta have dessert *here* some time. *We* eat them with cream and sugar."

4. Sitting in their room at the asylum, Whittle and Pare were distressed when the light bulb suddenly blew.

"Tarnation," said Whittle. "How're we supposed to read?"

"There's a spare bulb in the dresser," said Pare. "Why don't ya go up and change it?"

"How? We ain't got a ladder."

"No," said Pare, "but I've got a flashlight. I'll just turn it on and you kin climb up the beam."

"Sure," scoffed Whittle. "I'll be nearly to the top, and *bingo*! You'll turn it off!"


5. The asylum decided it would be good for the inmates to learn to work together. Thus they organized a baseball team, the star player of which was "Nuts" McGuirk. Unfortunately, though Nuts could slam the ball a mile and field like a demon, he had to be told what to do each and every step of the way. Thus, whenever Nuts had to play, the coach was always nearby.

The day of the first game arrived, and a large crowd gathered at a local stadium to see the lunatics play the doctors.

After nine innings it was a tie game. The inmates had the bases loaded, and there were two outs. Luckily, it was Nuts' turn to bat. The coach quietly whispered to him, "Up, Nuts!" and Nuts left the bench. "Bat, Nuts," he said, and the player went to the plate.

Alas, just then a vendor nearby shouted, "Peanuts!"

6. While being interviewed by a newspaper reporter, the asylum inmates were asked why
   they had been committed.

   Answered one: "We're all here because we're
   not all there."

**INSECTS**

*See also* MOTORCYCLE GANGS 2,
NYMPHOMANIACS 5,
RESTAURANTS 3, 4, 5, 6, 7, 8, 9, 10

1. Flitting over a pasture covered with cow shit,
   a pair of amorous flies spots a lone lady fly
   perched on a small chip.

   "And now," buzzed one of the flies, "watch
   as the foremost lover in all of flydom makes
   his move."

   Swooping down, he alit on a turd beside the
   female. Bowing low, he asked, "Pardon me,
   but is this stool taken?"

2. Encountering another cockroach dining under
   the sink, an insect says, "Have you heard about
   the new restaurant down the street? It's really
   something—the shelves are all spotless, the
   silverware is burnished to a high gloss, the
   appliances gleam— "

   "Please," the other roach says, holding up a
   leg, "not while I'm eating!"

3. The two weevils were born at the same time
   in the same cotton field, yet one was a success

and one was a dismal failure. Naturally, it wasn't long before the colony began referring to the latter creature as the lesser of two weevils. . . .

4. Then there were the newborn termites, also known as babes in the wood.

5. Finally, there were the two very competitive silkworms who had a race. It ended in a tie.

## INSOMNIA

1. "It's terrible," the man said to his friend. "I just lie in bed, staring at the ceiling, thinking about all the debts I have and all the things I have to get done at work. I swear, if I don't get some sleep soon, I'm going to lose my mind."

"You ought to do what I do," his friend said. "Take a few shots of whiskey or bourbon before you hit the sack."

"That makes you sleep?"

"Hell no," he said. "It makes you not mind being awake."

## INSURANCE

1. Reading of the marriage in the newspaper, the ambulance-chasing insurance agent drove out to the couple's house. When the husband an-

swered the door, the agent said, "Now that you're married, it would be wise to have more insurance."

The man turned and looked at his wife. "I don't see why," he said. "She doesn't look at all dangerous to me."


## INVENTIONS

*See also* ACCENTS 3

1. It was novel, if nothing else, and the patent officer reluctantly gave the Pole a patent on his solar-powered flashlight. . . .

2. Much to his surprise, when Josiah Barlett invented the thimble, his entire supply was sold out in a day. Naturally, he heard nothing but complaints from those who got stuck without one. . . .

3. Sitting around the bar one night, three men were discussing the strides humankind had made in the twentieth century.

   "If you ask me," said the first man, "the smartest invention of our time is the computer. Think of all the figuring and word processing it can do with the press of a button."

   The second man said, "The computer is smart, but it isn't as intelligent as a cruise missile. Imagine being able to follow a target wherever it goes."

   Shaking his head, the third man, a Pole,

said, "You're both way off base. The smartest invention of the twentieth century is the thermos."

The other two men looked at him and said in unison, "The thermos?"

"You bet. It keeps hot things hot, and cold things cold. Now tell me: how does it *know*?"

4. Then there was the chap who invented the circuit breaker. He was the only man in history who was delighted when people re-fused to use his product.

5. Needless to say, one of the most successful inventors of all time was the man who invented a hay-baling machine. He made a bundle.

6. Nearly as successful was the chemist who created a lubricant for furniture wheels, which he called caster oil.

7. Much less successful was the inventor of the pencil. After he used it for a few seconds, the lead snapped and he decided his invention was pointless.

8. As for the inventor of the relief map, all she got for her efforts was a small raise.

9. Finally, there was the august young man who invented fabric dye. As his grateful customers hailed the news: "Three cheers for thread, white and blue."

1. Q: What is gross stupidity?
   A: 144 Iranians.

2. Q: How do Iranian fishers count the day's haul?
   A: "One fish . . . two fish . . . another fish
   . . . another fish . . . another fish. . . ."

3. Q: Why doesn't the ayatollah get hemorrhoids?
   A: Because he's a perfect asshole.

4. Q: What do you call an Iranian with half a
   brain?
   A: Gifted.

5. Q: What do you call an Iranian who practices
   birth control?
   A: A humanitarian.

**THE IRISH**    *See also* ADAM AND EVE 2, PREJUDICE 12

1. Presenting his credentials to the president of
   the United States, the new ambassador from
   Ireland took umbrage to an offhanded remark
   the chief executive made about the problem of
   drunks in Ireland.
   "Beggin' yer pardon," said the Irishman,
   "but I daresay there are more drunks in Washington than in all of Ireland."

Stiffening, the president replied, "That's hogwash. In fact, you've got immunity. I dare you to go out and shoot the first fifty people you find who are drunk."

Accepting the challenge, the ambassador borrowed a gun and went outside.

The next day the Washington *Post* was emblazoned with the following headline: "AMBASSADOR SHOOTS FIFTY EMPLOYEES OF THE IRISH EMBASSY IN WASHINGTON!"

2. A Jew, a Frenchman, and an Irishman died and went to heaven. There they were met by St. Peter, who reviewed their records.

"You," he said to the Jew, "you liked money so much that you actually married a woman named Penny! Such a preoccupation with money is sinful, and we will not have your kind here."

His shoulders drooping, the Jew turned and began the long trek to hell.

Next, St. Peter opened the Frenchman's folder. "And you! You liked to drink so much that you sought out a wife by the name of Sherry! Alcohol too is a sin, and we will not have your kind here!"

Turning, the Frenchman headed toward hell, followed by the Irishman.

"Wait a minute," St. Peter called after him, "I haven't reviewed your file!"

"Why bother?" the Irishman said. "My wife's name was Fanny."

3. Then there's the Irish version of a queer—someone who prefers women to liquor.

## THE IRS

1. Q: What do you need when you have an IRS auditor buried to his neck in concrete?
   A: More concrete.

2. Q: What's the difference between a pothole and an IRS agent?
   A: You'd swerve to avoid the pothole.

3. Answering the phone, the priest was surprised to hear the caller introduce herself as an IRS auditor.

   "But we don't pay taxes," the priest said.

   "It isn't you, Father, it's one of your parishioners, Sean McCullough. He indicates on his tax return that he gave a donation of $15,000 to the church last year. Is this, in fact, the truth?"

   The priest smiled broadly. "The check hasn't arrived yet, but I'm sure I'll have it when I remind dear Sean."

4. "That's precisely the point," the IRS auditor said to an irate taxpayer, "we *do* intend to make a federal case out of it."

**JAPANESE**    *See also* ACCENTS 8, CHILDBIRTH 1,
DOGS 2, JEWISH AMERICAN PRINCESSES 8,
ORGASMS 2, WORLD WAR II 2

1. Eiji was thrilled when his wife went into labor. Much to his surprise, however, the baby came out with blue, straight eyes, blond hair, and light skin.

    "How could this be?" Eiji exclaimed. "How can my baby be white?"

    Shrugging, his wife said, "Occidents will happen."

2. Eiji and his wife had friends named the Wongs. Mr. Wong was just as surprised as Eiji when his wife also bore a child which looked nothing like any Oriental *he'd* ever seen. Unlike Eiji, however, Mr. Wong sued for divorce, which the judge immediately granted. As he put it, "There was obviously some hanky-panky going on, since two Wongs don't make a white."

**JESUS CHRIST**    *See also* CLERGY,
EVANGELISTS, GOD, HEAVEN, GOLF 2

1. Following the Star of Bethlehem, the three wise men approached the manger in which Mary, Joseph, and their babe were seated.

    As he walked in, one of the wise men stepped on a goat turd. "Jesus *Christ!*" he roared.

Mary brightened and looked at Joseph. "Dear, what do you think of *that* instead of Melvin?"

2. Pushing his way to the front of the crowd, Jesus waved his arms in front of the mad throng. When they had quieted, he helped up a woman whom they had been pelting with stones.

"This is wrong! Let he who is without sin cast the first stone."

Suddenly a rock came flying from the midst of the mob, and caught the woman square in the forehead.

Peering across the sea of faces, Jesus swore. "Dammit! Is that you again, Mother?"

3. Curious to see how civilization had changed in two thousand years, Jesus returned to earth incognito. He went to the movies, ate at restaurants, attended the theater, and drove modern automobiles. When he returned to heaven, St. Peter asked him how he enjoyed his trip.

"It was splendid!" he said. "The movies are most artistic, the restaurants have no-smoking sections, the musicals are spectacular, and the automobiles have computer controls! There's one thing I regret, though," he said reflectively.

"What's that?" St. Peter asked.

"I would have liked to try the confection called M&Ms. It is said they do not melt in your hands."

"Were these confections unavailable while you were there?" St. Peter asked.

"No," Jesus replied, glancing mournfully at his hands. "They kept slipping through the holes."

## JEWISH AMERICAN PRINCESSES

See also JEWS, BASEBALL 4

1. At a party a man looked in his drink and said, "Now isn't that cute. Ice cubes with holes in them."

   "That's nothing," said the man standing next to him. "I've been married to one for ten years!"

2. Legend has it that there was once a Jewish nymphomaniac: she had to have a man every six months.

3. On the other hand, there was a man who knew the night was going to be a washout. As they sat necking on the couch, he asked his date why she wasn't responding. When she opened her mouth to answer, a little light went on. . . .

4. Q: If Tarzan and Jane were Jewish, what would that make Cheeta?
   A: A fur coat.

5. Q: Why do JAPs were bikinis?
   A: To separate the milk from the fish.

6. Q: What's six inches long, has a bald head, and drives Jewish women wild?
   A: A hundred-dollar bill.

7. Q: What's the difference between an Italian woman and a Jewish woman?
   A: One has real orgasms and fake diamonds. . . .

8. Q: What do you get when you cross a Jap and a JAP?
   A: An Orienta.

9. Waiting in the maternity room, an Irishman, a Japanese man, and a Jew jump up as the nurse enters. She's carrying a black baby in her arms.
   "Is it yours?" she asks the Irishman.
   "Definitely not," he replies.
   "Is it yours?" she asks the Japanese.
   He shakes his head.
   "Could it be yours?" she asks the Jew.
   "Probably," he sighs. "My wife burns everything."

10. Worst of all was the JAP whose husband was convinced that she was magnetic. After all, everything she touched, she charged.

11. Lastly, there was the JAP who was so sexually inhibited that she was tied up in nots.

1. Called in by the KGB for questioning, the old
   Jew was told to sit in a chair in a bare room.
   
   "You are suspected of plotting against the
   Soviet Union," said the agent who had brought
   him in. "However, you can redeem yourself
   by answering a few questions. For example,
   who was Karl Marx?"
   
   The Jew shrugged. "Never heard of him."
   
   "Lenin?"
   
   "Don't know."
   
   The agent frowned. "Are you toying with
   me?"
   
   "Certainly not!" said the Jew. "Do you know
   Shlomo Schatzman?"
   
   "No."
   
   "Or Mordecai Tischler?"
   
   "No—"
   
   "You see?" said the Jew. "You've got your
   friends, and I've got mine."

2. Q: How many Jewish mothers does it take to
      screw in a lightbulb?
   A: None. "It's all right. I'll sit here in the
      dark."

3. After spending nearly a half-century in hell,
   Hitler was ordered to visit the earth for twenty-

four hours and see what had been built in his absence. After just two hours Hitler was back, pounding on Hades' gates.

"Let me in!" he screamed.

The devil came to see him. "What's wrong? Aren't you impressed with the way the world has recovered from the horror you wrought?"

"Impressed?" Hitler demanded. "Everything's all backward!"

"Backward?" the devil asked.

"Yes! It's the Jews who are fighting and the Germans who are making money!"

4. Q: What's a Jewish catch-22?
   A: Free pork.

5. The Russian, the Englishman, and the Jew were visited in their cell in Stalingrad by their German captors.

"All right," the *leutnant* said, "each of you may have a last wish before you are shot."

The Russian said, "I would like to make my confession." The officer obliged him and brought in a priest.

The Englishman said, "I would like to have a cigarette." The officer obliged him and gave him a smoke.

The Jew said, "I would like to have some strawberries."

"*Schwein!*" shouted the German. "There are no strawberries in the dead of winter!"

"Fine," said the Jew, sitting back down. "I'll wait."

6. During the days of the tsar, a Jew plunged into the Moscow River.

   "Help!" he cried to two passing soldiers. "I can't swim!"

   "Then drown, you heathen!" one shouted back.

   Thinking quickly, the Jew shouted, "Down with Nicholas!"

   Without hesitation the soldiers jumped in, dragged him out, and arrested him for sedition.

7. Then there was the Talmudic scholar who wondered how this could possibly be a Christian world when the sun is named Sol.

## JOAN OF ARC                 *See also* AUTOMOBILES 2

1. Q: Why did Joan of Arc cancel her date with a ravishing Frenchman?
   A: Because she already had a date with a Pole.

2. Q: What's the difference between an igloo and Joan of Arc?
   A: One is made of ice, the other Maid of Orleans.

## JOGGERS

1. Q: What's the difference between a sewing machine and a lady jogging?
   A: The sewing machine has just one bobbin.

1. Len, joke teller *extraordinaire*, was holding court at the local pub.

   "So the train pulls into the station, and these two Jews get off—"

   Suddenly a man shouts, "Hold on!" and gets up from his stool. "I'm Jewish, and I'm sick and tired of hearing jokes about 'Two Jews were *this*,' and 'Two Jews were *that*.' Christ, man, pick on some other people for a change!"

   Willing to oblige, Len clears his throat and says, "So the train pulls into the station, and these two Eskimos get off. And one says, 'So, there we were, at my son's bar mitzvah. . . .'"

2. Q: Why is a joke like a pussy?
   A: Neither is any fun if you don't get it.

3. Q: Why are consumer advocates generally so humorless?
   A: They can't recall a joke.

**JOURNALISM** *See also* CIRCUS 1

1. Tucker, the newspaper magnate, spent nearly a half-million dollars to buy himself a race horse. Unimpressed, farmer Jones offered to race his horse against the thoroughbred. The entire town gathered for the event, including

reporters from all of Tucker's newspapers. Unfortunately for the magnate, his horse lost by a wide margin.

The following day the sports pages of all of Tuckers' papers were emblazoned with the headline, "TUCKER'S HORSE COMES IN SECOND, JONES' HORSE IS NEXT-TO-LAST."

2. Then there was the gossip columnist who was proud to be writing others' wrongs.


## KANGAROOS

1. Bursting with nationalistic pride, an enterpreneur announced plans to set up shop in the Outback and make the first Australian beer. Two months later, he was visited by a friend. The new arrival was shocked to see him sitting beside a vat in the middle of a plain, without a single finished keg of beer.

"What the bleedin' hell are you doing?" the friend asked.

"What d'ya think?" asked the entrepreneur. "Waitin' for the kangaroos."

"Kangaroos? What in God's name for?"

"What else?" asked the man. "The hops."

2. Then there was the exhausted kangaroo who stopped out of bounds.

1. Like human children, the whisk broom demanded to know whence she came. Blushing a little, her mother said, "Your father and I swept together."

2. Mr. and Mrs. Piccard smiled knowingly as their seven-year-old son, Lance, talked about the afternoon he spent with his playmate Wendy.

    "Y'know, Dad," the boy said, "I think Wendy and I are going to get married."

    "That's very nice," Mr. Piccard said, "but don't you think you ought to wait? After all, you're seven and Wendy's six. How will you pay your bills?"

    Without missing a beat, Lance replied, "The way we figured it, if we pool our allowance, and shovel a few extra driveways each winter, we'll make out just fine."

    Mrs. Piccard chuckled. "And what will you do when you have children?"

    Lance looked up. "So far," he says, "we've been real lucky."

3. Running into the house after school, a little boy said to his mother, "Mom! Isn't an ox a kind of a bull?"

"Yes—"

"And doesn't equine have something to do with horses?"

"That's right."

The boy ran from the kitchen. "I'll see you later!"

"Why? Where are you going?"

"To some other town. I just heard in school that the equinox is coming, and I don't wanna be around when it gets here!"

4. Walking over to her son, the woman said, "Here's sixty cents. Why don't you go to the grocer's and get yourself a Coke."

"Gee, thanks!" said the boy. "What about Terry? Can I ask him to go too?"

"Sure," said the mother, handing him another sixty cents. "You can both get yourself Cokes."

"And what about Terry's sister? Sometimes she likes to go with us."

"Here's sixty cents more, for another Coke," the mother smiled. Then she handed him a twenty-dollar bill and a shopping list. "And while you're there, would you mind picking up just a few things for me?"

The moral: Kids will do whatever you want if you coax them enough.

5. Moving into a new neighborhood, Michael tried to impress the other kids in his class.

"My granddad's got a wooden leg and can unscrew it," he said proudly.

stealing money. Flying from Sicily, he has all of his young lieutenants brought in one at a time. Alone in a room with his translator Maria, he asks each of them if they have been taking money. Whenever a man says no, the don puts a gun to the man's head. If he still says no, the don lets him go.

The last lieutenant brought before the don is Salvatore, and he's shaking like a leaf.

"So," says the don through his translator, "are you the one who has been stealing from me?"

"No, Godfather," says the man.

The godfather puts the pistol to the man's temple. "I ask you again: are you the one who has been stealing from me?"

Quaking horribly, the man screams, "Yes! Yes! I took the money and put it in a suitcase in my attic!"

The don looks at his translator.

"Godfather," she reports, "he says, 'I'll bet this old fart doesn't have the balls to pull the trigger.' "

6. While touring the South, an English teacher from New York stopped to chat with the locals in a country store.

"Yeah," said a man, "muh wife an' I are repairin' tuh take a trip north tuh visit fam'ly."

Smiling, the teacher said, "I don't mean to be rude, but you mean that you're preparing to take a trip north. Repairing means *fixing*."

"That's whut I said," the southerner went on, "muh wife an' I are repairin' tuh take a trip north."

7. Q: Do black people really talk funny?
   A: No. It be a miff.

8. English, of course, is a language of strict rules. For example, double negatives are a no-no. . . .

## LAVATORIES

*See also* DEFECATION, SEPTIC TANKS, DOCTORS 1, DRUNKS 1, THE HANDICAPPED 1

1. After a night of drinking, Jim had a rather full bladder. He asked the bartender for directions to the men's room.

   "You go to the back, turn to your right, turn left, then go in the first door on the left."

   Setting out, Jim turned right, then left, then made the mistake of walking through the first door on the right. Instead of entering the men's room, he fell swiftly and painfully down an elevator shaft which was undergoing repairs.

   Hearing his shouts, another patron hurried over. "Hey, fella! Are you all right?"

   "I am," Jim shouted back, "but *whatever* you do—don't flush!"

2. On his first trip to the United States an Arab potentate was treated to a formal White House

dinner. Unaccustomed to the salty foods, but not wishing to offend his hosts, he had his aide slip quietly away and bring him constant refills for his water glass.

After a lengthy time away, the aide returned without water. Furious, the potentate demanded to know where it was.

Bowing low, the aide said, "Forgive me, Your Majesty, but we must wait: Secretary of State is sitting on well."

3. Q: What does the sign say in the Polish restroom?
   A: Please don't eat the mints.

4. While traveling through the deep South, a salesperson stopped at an inn for a meal. When he was through, he asked to use the bathroom. The proprietor pointed to an outhouse in the back.

   After moving his bowels, the man found, to his chagrin, that there was no toilet paper. Instead there was a small hole in the wall, a slot, and a sign. The sign read, "Insert twenty-five cents and your dirty finger will be cleaned with the greatest care, warmth, and attention."

   Unhappy but having no other choice, the man used his finger to clean himself, plugged a quarter into the slot, then put his finger in the hole.

   Unknown to him, a little boy was standing on the other side with a pair of bricks. When the finger came through, the lad smashed it between the bricks; howling with pain, the man poked the finger into his mouth.

5. Q: If an American goes into the bathroom, and an American comes out of the bathroom, what are you in between?
   A: European.


## LAWYERS

See also COURTROOMS, DIVORCE, AUTOMOBILE ACCIDENTS 1, DRUGS 2, EXECUTION 4, HEAVEN 4, MARRIAGE 9, SODOMY 5, WILLS 2, 3, 4

1. Q: What's the difference between a lawyer and a vulture?
   A: Lawyers can take off their wingtips.

2. Q: What's the difference between a suit of clothes and a law suit?
   A: One gets cleaned and pressed for the client. As for the other, when it gets pressed, it's the client who gets cleaned.

3. While visiting the cemetery, the grieving couple noticed a headstone which read, "HERE LIES A LAWYER AND AN HONEST MAN."
   "Look at that," said the woman, "money s so tight they're putting them two in a grave."

4. Explaining the fee structure to a client, the attorney said, "What a contingent fee means is

that if we lose your suit, I get nothing. And if
we win, you get nothing."

5. After being arrested for robbery, Quinn hired
   the best lawyer in town.
   "Look," the crook said, "I've got nearly a
   million in cash in my bank box. Can you get
   me off?"
   The lawyer said, "Believe me, pal, you'll
   never go to prison with that kind of money."
   And sure enough, he did not. He went to
   prison flat broke.

6. Then there was the attorney who introduced
   herself to her client as a criminal lawyer.
   The client commended her for being so
   self-aware.

7. Another attorney was even more candid: he
   described himself as a man who helps you get
   what's coming to him.

8. Finally, there was the attorney who worked
   day and night just to break the young widow's
   will. . . .

9. Perhaps, when all is said and done, lawyers
   deserve a high fee because they *are* such a
   unique breed. Who but an attorney can read a
   thirty-page document and call it a "brief"?

1. "You've got to help me," said the leper as he shambled into Dr. Cohen's office. "My dick just fell off!"

    "Give it to me, quickly," Cohen said. "We may be able to save it through microsurgery."

    "It's in my coat pocket," the leper said.

    The doctor reached in. "Hell, man, this is a cigar!"

    The leper paled. "Jesus H. Christ—I just smoked my cock!"

2. Q: How does a leper get out of a poker game?
   A: He throws in his hand.

3. Q: Why were the lepers kicked off the soccer team?
   A: Because they were defeated.

4. Another miserable soul was the pitcher who was forced to retire from the leper colony baseball team after he threw his arm out.

5. It was unfortunate, but the coach also had to dismiss his leper outfielder when the poor fellow dropped two balls.

6. As if that weren't bad enough, the NFL's only leper quarterback had to be put on waivers. There was a handoff on the very first play.

7. Then there was the leper who found out she was also epileptic, and went to pieces.

8. Equally pathetic was the leper who went to New York and had her kneecaps stolen.

9. . . . and the leper who failed her driver's test. Seems she left her foot on the gas. . . .

10. . . . and the horny leper who made the painful mistake of jerking off. . . .

## LIBRARIES

1. "So there I was," said the student, "studying, when all of a sudden the librarian sits on my hand!"

   "Old Miss Grinch?" said a friend. "What did you do?"

   "What *could* I do? I got her off."

## LIFESTYLE

1. "Hymie," whined his wife, Jessica, "you know that hat you bought me last week? Well, Mrs. Nadoolman across the street bought one just like it."

   Hymie looked up from his newspaper. "I see. And now I suppose you want me to buy you a new one."

"Well," she said, "it would be a lot cheaper than moving."

2.  The irony of keeping up with the Joneses, of course, is that you spend money you don't have to buy things you don't need to impress people you don't like.

3.  The Frenchman, the German, and the Israeli were standing around in the cafe in Tel Aviv, comparing their lifestyles.

    "When I go to work," said the Frenchman, "I drive my Renault. On weekends I drive my $30,000 Peugeot. And when I travel aboard, I always drive a $50,000 Citroen."

    "Bah," said the German, "I drive a Volkswagen to work. But on weekends I drive a $50,000 BMW, and when I go abroad, I always take my customized $60,000 Mercedes."

    "Very impressive," the Israeli admitted. "As for me, I take the bus to work, and on Sundays I motor around in my little Ford. But when *I* go abroad, I drive a $250,000 tank."

4.  "I've discovered," said the in-debt-to-the-eyeballs consumer, "that credit cards are nothing but a quick way to boost my yearning capacity."

5.  And, of course, the person who puts food on the table is called the breadwinner. They're called that because today the only way anyone can afford to eat is by winning the lottery.

1. Q: How many Californians does it take to screw
      in a lightbulb.
   A: None. Californians only screw in hot tubs.

2. Q: How many pessimists does it take to screw
      in a lightbulb?
   A: None. "The burned-out one is probably
      screwed in too tight."

3. Q: How many sex therapists does it take to
      screw in a light bulb?
   A: Two. One to screw it in, and one to tell
      him he's screwing all wrong.

4. Q: How many feminists does it take to change
      a light bulb?
   A: Three. One to change the bulb, another to
      write about how the socket is being ex-
      ploited, and a third, watching them, who
      secretly wishes that *she* were the socket.

5. As a publicity stunt, a light-bulb salesperson
   advertises that he will give free bulbs to a
   movie theater owner who uses them on the
   marquee.
      Or, as the salesperson put it, "I've always
   wanted to see my lights up in names."

1. While walking from one village to another, a missionary takes a shortcut and becomes hopelessly lost. Making his way through the jungle, he encounters a large and very hungry lion.

   Turning, the missionary runs, with the lion in hot pursuit. Finally the man of the cloth runs smack up against a mountain cliff. Trapped by the carnivore, he drops to the ground and begins to pray.

   Suddenly the lion also gets on its knees and folds it paws.

   "A miracle!" the missionary exclaims. "God has caused you to join one of his lambs in prayer instead of slaughtering him!"

   Suddenly the lion looks up. "Will you shut your trap? I'm saying grace."

2. The lion tamer led his young apprentice into the cage. "The first thing to remember," said the older man, "is that if a lion jumps at you, throw something at it."

   "And what do I do if there's nothing to throw?"

   The lion tamer said, "If a lion jumps at you—there *will* be."

3. While stalking through the jungle, the lioness spotted two men sitting at the edge of the

veldt. One was reading a newspaper; the other working feverishly over a manual typewriter.

With a bound the lioness leapt on the man with the newspaper, and ate him up. However, she let the other man go free, for as every predator knows, readers digest but writers cramp.

## LITERATURE

*See also* GOATS 1

1. While admitting it was a masterpiece, the school board had no choice but to ban *Ivanhoe* from English classes. The reason? As one prude put it, "Too much Saxon violence."

2. Q: What do you call a little wooden boy whose nuts grow each time he tells a lie?
   A: Pistachio.

3. Q: How did Captain Hook die?
   A: He forgot himself, and wiped with the wrong hand.

4. After watching Little Red Riding Hood leave her home, the wolf hurried through the woods and broke into the home of the little girl's grandmother.

   "Awright, granny," snarled the animal, "get outta bed. I'm gonna lock you in the closet!"

   Reaching under her pillow, the elderly woman withdrew a shotgun. "Oh no, you're not, big fella," she said, spreading her legs. "You're gonna do just like the story says."

5. Q: How does *A Tale of Two Titties* open?
   A: "It was the bust of times. . . ."

6. Then there was the psychiatrist who analyzed Dickens's *A Christmas Carol* and concluded that the root of Scrooge's problems was a severe case of Claustrophobia. . . .

7. Q: What do you call negroes who read *The Hobbit?*
   A: Tolkien blacks.

## LOGIC                    *See also* IMMIGRANTS 1, NUMBERS 1

1. Logical Isaac Spock went up to the bar and ordered a double scotch. Familiar with Spock's reputation around town, the bartender tapped the bar and said, "I'm pouring nothing, pal, until you put your money on the table."

   Since Spock didn't have a penny, he said, "Listen, you got a cat here?"

   "Sure."

   "Okay. I'll bet you a drink that my dong is longer than your cat's tail."

   Snickering, the bartender fetched his calico and a ruler, and measured the competing members. When he was through, he looked Spock square in the eye.

190

"Pay up or ship out. This cat's got you beat by three inches!"

Spock scratched his head. "That can't be. Tell me, just where did you *begin* measuring that cat's tail."

"From its arse, of course."

Spock rose in triumph. "I would appreciate, sir, if you'd now show *me* the same courtesy."

2. Walking down Main Street during a fierce wind, Lou was shocked to see an old woman with her hands on her head and her dress swirling up around them, exposing her privates.

As she approached, he said, "You ought to be ashamed of yourself!"

"Look," snapped the woman, "all that stuff is seventy-two years old. But this *hat* is brand-new!"

3. "Dammit," said another pedestrian while waiting for the light to change.

"What's wrong?" asked his companion.

"My watch stopped when it hit the pavement back there."

"Naturally," said the other. "You didn't expect it to go clear through, did you?"

4. "Hey, Spiro," said the man down the bar, "what time is it?"

Looking up from his double scotch, Spiro said, "I couldn't say fer sure, Morty—but I do know that it ain't three o'clock."

"How do you know that?"

" 'Cause I told my wife I'd be home by then, and I ain't there."

## LUMBER

1. Chatting with the owner of the lumberyard, the builder asked how business was doing.

   Moving his hand back and forth, the owner said, "Come see, come saw."

## MAIDS

1. While teaching a weekly art class the instructor said, "I know of a painter who was so meticulous that he rendered a cobweb on the wall, and his cleaning lady spent an hour trying to get it off."

   "That's ridiculous," said one of the students, a housewife.

   "Not at all," the teacher replied. "If you spend enough time here, you will be able to draw anything you wish, as realistically as you wish. Artists have been known to do such things to hone their craft."

   "Artists perhaps," she said. "But not cleaning women."

2. Then there's the sage who insists that a wife made-to-order can't hold a candle to one ready-maid.

## MARRIAGE

*See also* MOTHER-IN-LAW,
AUTOMOBILE ACCIDENTS 2, CANNIBALS 3,
GOLF 5, INSURANCE 2, SEX 14, 20,
WILLS 2, 3, 5

1. Despite being a superb shot with the bow and arrow, it's amazing that Cupid has made so many bad Mrs.

2. Gwen was shocked when her twenty-two-year-old friend Peggy announced one day that she was going to marry a seventy-two-year-old man.

   "Peggy," she said, "you know these May-December marriages are never happy ones for May. December finds energy and beauty and youth in May, but what does May *ever* find in December?"

   Winking, Peggy replied, "Santa."

3. While reading the newspaper, Morty came across an article about a beautiful actress marrying a football player who was not noted for his IQ.

   "I'll never understand," he said to his wife, "why the biggest jerks get the most attractive wives."

   His wife replied, "Why, thank you, dear."

4. The angry wife met her husband at the door. There was alcohol on his breath, and lipstick on his cheek.

"I assume," she snarled, "that there is a *very* good reason for you to come waltzing in at five o'clock in the morning!"

"There is," he replied. "Breakfast."

5. During one of their typically violent arguments, Mr. Robbins lost control and began beating Mrs. Robbins. Just then the local priest happened to walk in the door.

Spotting the clergyman, Mr. Robbins stood back and said, "*Now*, Agatha, will you go with me to mass?"

6. Upon returning home from two years fighting the Germans in occupied France, Max came home. Walking in the door, he endeavored to impress his ever-grumpy wife with the French he'd learned.

"*Je t'adore!*" he said as he crossed the threshold.

From the kitchen his wife yelled, "Lazy bum! Shut it yourself!"

7. At Rod's stag party his father raised a glass and proposed a toast. "To my son, on the happiest day of his life."

"But, Pop," Rod said, "I'm not getting married until tomorrow."

Said the old man: "I repeat. To my son. . . ."

8. Then there's the battle-hardened spouse who points out that while the cooing ends on the wedding night, the billing goes on forever. . . .

9. And while it's true that more women than ever are taking up the law and becoming lawyers, the large majority are still laying down the law and becoming wives.

10. Walking into the bar, Harvey said to the bartender, "Pour me a stiff one, Eddie. I just had another fight with the little woman."

   "Oh yeah?" Eddie said. "And how did *this* one end."

   "When it was over," Harvey replied, "my wife came to me on her hands and knees."

   "Really? Now there's a switch! What did she say."

   "She said, 'Come out from under that bed, you gutless weasel!' "

## MASOCHISTS

1. Q: When do masochists laugh?
   A: Whenever anything strikes them funny.

## MASTURBATION

See also SEX, FOOTBALL 1, LEPERS 10

1. Q: Why is sex like bridge?
   A: If you have a good hand, you don't need a partner.

2. As he did every year, Mr. Wilson went out and shot a turkey for Thanksgiving dinner.

Unfortunately, this year he was forced to use buckshot instead of his regular ammunition.

After dinner Mrs. Wilson suddenly bolted from the table and ran to the bathroom. When she returned, she said, "Dear, what were those black stones floating in my pee?"

"Oh," said Mr. Wilson, "that's just buckshot. Guess I didn't get it all when I cleaned the turkey."

A few minutes later, Grandpa Wilson ran to the bathroom. When he returned, he snapped, "Jesus, I had buckshot in my stool. I wish you'd've warned us, sonny!"

Just then young Billy Wilson came running downstairs. "Daddy, Daddy," he yelled, "I'm sorry."

"What's wrong?" Mrs. Wilson asked.

"I—I was whacking off and I shot the dog!"

3. Q: What do you call a medieval masturbator?
   A: A pounding serf.

4. Having lunch one day, a sex therapist said to her friend, "According to a survey we just completed, ninety percent of all people masturbate in the shower. Only ten percent of them sing."

"Really?"

The therapist nodded. "And do you know what song they sing?"

The friend shook her head.

The therapist said, "I didn't think so."

5. Q: What happened when the man with no arms tried to masturbate?
A: He was stumped.

6. Then there was the soldier who was stationed on a remote South Pacific island with nary a woman inhabitant. It was nearly two years before the poor fellow received an honorable discharge. . . .

7. . . . and the man who satisfied himself onboard a commercial airliner and was arrested for skyjacking.

8. Q: If lovers celebrate Valentine's Day, what do lonely men celebrate?
A: Palm Sunday.

## MEDICAL SCHOOL
*See also* ACCENTS 6

1. "To succeed in medicine nowadays, there are two things every doctor needs," the instructor told his medical students. "The first is gray hair. That will make you look wise and responsible."

"And the second thing?" asked a student.

"Hemorrhoids," the instructor said, "to give you a look of concern."

1. The Mexicans were delighted when a bridge was built across the Rio Grande. At last they could swim across in the shade.

2. Q: Why didn't Mexico have a team in the 1984 Olympics in Los Angeles?
   A: Because every Mexican who could jump, run, or swim was already there.

3. Then there was the Mexican homosexual who insisted on being referred to as a senoreater.

**THE MILITARY**       *See also* COURT-MARTIALS, THE FOREIGN LEGION, WEST POINT, WORLD WAR II, MASTURBATION 6, MORONS 5, MUSSOLINI 3, TAMPONS 2, VENERAL DISEASES 3, WORDPLAY 3

1. After enlisting in the army, Marvin had second thoughts about serving. Thus, when he was told to bring a urine sample to the selective service medical office, he filled a bottle with specimens from his father, sister, dog, and then a bit of his own.

   Striding confidently into the lab, he waited for a full hour while the sample was analyzed. Finally the technician strode in.

   "It took some doing," she said, "but according to our analysis, your father has the clap, your sister is pregnant, your dog is in heat, and you're in the army."

2. Because of budget cuts, Major Price received his orders and dutifully carried them out. A week later, he was called in to see General Attwood.

The general said, "According to these reports, there are *still* as many men at Fort Drake as when I told you to reduce your staff!" He looked up. "What in hell's going on there?"

"Reduce my staff?" Price said, gulping hard and rubbing the top of his head. "Sir, when you said we all needed crew cuts, I thought. . . ."

## MISERS

1. Mr. Fingers, head of a local charity, was annoyed because no one had ever gotten Mr. Crump, one of the wealthiest men in the town, to contribute to their cause. Arranging to visit the millionaire in his office, Mr. Fingers said, "Sir, according to our research, you earned over one million dollars last year. Would it hurt you to give us just a little of that so we can continue our good work?"

Crump leaned forward on his desk. "Mr. Fingers. Does your research show that I have a widowed mother who has no source of income? Or a sister whose husband drowned in a boating accident and has three little children to support? Or a mother-in-law whose husband ran off with every penny she had. Or a brother who lost his arms in a car crash?" He sat back. "Well, sir, if I don't give to them, why should I give to you?"

## MISTRESSES

*See also* MARRIAGE, SEX

1. Meeting his mistress for dinner, the married man said, "Answer me this, my dear—what would you do if you found yourself pregnant and abandoned?"

   "Why," she said, "I—I think I'd kill myself!"

   Sitting back, the man sighed, "Good girl."

2. After making love to his mistress, the mayor of East Berlin was surprised when she turned to him and said, "Hans, why don't we give the people their wish and dismantle that ugly Wall?"

   Pinching her cheek, the mayor said playfully, "So, my little *schätze*, you want it to be just me and you!"

## MOBILE HOMES

1. After years of boom, the realtor couldn't sell a single house. Turning to mobile homes, he became instead a wheel-estate agent. . . .

## MORONS
*See also* ACTORS 6, BANKING 2,
CLOTHING 1, CONDOMS 4, CRIME 2, DEFECATION 1,
DIVORCE 5, FISHING 2, GAMBLING 2, HUNTERS 1, 2, 3, 4,
INDUSTRY 2, MOTION PICTURES 4, PARTIES 2,
THE POST OFFICE 1, 2, SEX 27, SHOES 2,
SUN DIALS 1, TOURISTS 3, 4,
VENEREAL DISEASES 3, WALLPAPER 1, WEST POINT 1

1. Carrying on with another man's wife, the moron went to a motel for an afternoon tryst. After he signed the register, the clerk looked down.

   "I've seen people sign their names with an 'X'," the clerk said, "but never an 'X' with a box around it."

   The moron replied, "Sometimes, pal, a person just don't want t'use his real name."

2. Gustav the builder was rushed to the hospital, his foot wrapped in bandages and bleeding profusely.

   "What happened?" demanded the intern.

   Gustav put his hand to his head. "Doc, twenty years ago, when I was learnin' my trade in Oslo, I was—"

   "Twenty years ago? What about your *foot*, man?"

   "I'm gettin' to that. Anyway, I was learnin' my trade, apprenticing with a builder named Norstrom and livin' in his house. The night I arrived, his beautiful daughter came over wearin' a short nightgown an' said t'me, 'Is there anything I can do for you, Gustav?' An' I said, 'No, thank you. I have everything I need.'

"The next night she came back wearin' the same short nightgown and perfume that made her smell like a rose. An' she said, 'Is there *anything* I can do for you, Gustav?' An' I said, 'No, thank you. I have everything I need.'

"The followin' night she came in stark naked and asked me again, 'Is there anything at *all* I can do for you, Gustav?' An' I said, 'No, thank you. I have everything I need.'"

The doctor sighed. "What does that have to do with your *foot*?"

Gustav scowled. "Well, this mornin', sir, I finally figured out what she meant, and got so angry that I threw down a hammer and busted my foot!"

3. Walking up to the owner of the apple orchard, the moron asked, "How much do you charge for apples?"

"All you can pick for five bucks."

"Fine," said the moron, reaching into his pocket, "I'll take ten dollars' worth."

4. Filling out a job application, the moron was stumped when he came to the box marked "SEX." After checking "M" and "F," he wrote in the margin, "Sometimes we screw on Wednesday, too."

5. The hillbilly wasn't very smart, but he was patriotic. As soon as his son was born, he took him to the nearest army recruiter.

    "Now what do you expect us to do with him?" asked the sergeant.

    "Why, heck," the hillbilly replied, "put him in the infantry, ya durn fool."

6. Overwhelmed by the amount of work he had to do, the moron cut his correspondence classes. He sent in empty envelopes.

7. Q: Why did the moron sell his water skis?
   A: He couldn't find a lake on a slope.

8. While walking through Sears, the moron saw a photographer doing portraits of children.

    "How much?" the moron asked.

    "It's fifteen dollars for four," the photographer said.

    "It figures," the moron sighed. "I've only got two."

9. Then there was the moron who had his finger broken when someone punched him in the nose.

10. Later that day, that same moron brought a ladder to the party because he'd heard that drinks were on the house.

11. Which wasn't as bad as the moron whose wife asked him to change their baby daughter. He returned an hour later with a black boy.

12. . . . or the moron who got on his knees in front of the deli so he could practice hero worship.

## MOTHERS-IN-LAW

1. "Why I didn't listen to Mother, I'll never know!" screamed Mrs. Shooter. "She *told* me not to marry you!"

   Mr. Shooter put down the book he was about to throw. "Your mother said that?"

   "She did!"

   "Christ," Shooter said. "How I've *misjudged* that woman all these years!"

2. After witnessing his friend McGilley push his mother-in-law from the fifth-floor window, the police officer ran upstairs.

   "Why did you do that?"

   "I'm sorry! I—I did it without thinking!"

   "I'll say! You might have hurt someone passing below!"

## MOTION PICTURES
See also ACTORS, MUSSOLINI 2, THE POLISH 6, 7

1. "Gee, Mr. Speelberger," gushed the starlet, "do you really think I have a chance of being a big star?"

   The producer replied, "My dear, you're already making it big."

2. Another of the women coveted by the lascivious filmmaker was told in no uncertain terms that she'd never be a star until she got her "no's" fixed.

3. Then there was the successful motion picture director who couldn't resist making a little extra on the side.

4. Q: Why did nineteen morons go to the movies?
   A: Because the sign out front said, "UNDER EIGHTEEN NOT ADMITTED."

## MOTORCYCLE GANGS

1. Lying in the hospital ward after piling his motorcycle into the back of a truck, the Hell's Angel had a visit from his doctor.

   "Well, Brutus, I have good news and bad news," the physician said. "The bad news is that I'm going to have to amputate your legs."

   "Sheeeeit!" the biker swore. "What the hell's the good news?"

   "See that gentleman in the bed over there? He wants to buy your boots."

2. Q: How can you tell when a biker is happy?
   A: There are bugs in his teeth.

1. Q: What did they call the episode of *The Muppets* in which Miss Piggy whacked Kermit in the balls?
   A: "Green Achers."

## MURDER

*See also* DEATH, DATING 2, HOMOSEXUALS 5, INFIDELITY 1, TOPLESS BARS 3, MOTHERS-IN-LAW 2

1. The inspector was examining the pistol. "Officer O'Hara, you say the woman plugged her husband at close range."

   "Yes, sir."

   The inspector looked down at the body. "Are there any powder marks?"

   O'Hara replied, "Yes, sir. That's why she blew him away."

2. Walking down the street with a hatbox under his arm, Jacob was stopped by an acquaintance.

   "Jake! What've you got there, a gift for the little woman?"

   "No," Jake answered, and opened the box. Inside was a woman's head nestled inside a large straw hat with plastic flowers and green-and-pink band.

   "Christ," the man said, "that's horrible."

   Said Jake, "Y'know, that's exactly what *I*

told her when she said she paid two hundred dollars for it."

3. Suspecting that his wife was having an affair, a man hid down the street to make certain. Sure enough, less than an hour after he left home, a handsome young stud walked in the door. Furious, the husband hired a hit man to shoot them to death.

"It's five thousand dollars a shot," the killer pointed out.

"I don't care," the irate husband said, "as long as you do what I want. I want my wife shot in the head, and the man's dick shot off."

Later, the husband got a call from the killer at work.

"This is your lucky day," he said. "It'll only cost you five grand."

"Why?" the husband said. "Didn't you get them both?"

"I did," he said, "but I was able to do it in one shot."

**MUSIC**   See also NICARAGUA 2, PSYCHIATRISTS 1,
ROCK AND ROLL 2, 4, RUSSIANS 15

1. A down-and out musician, Dunwiddy was playing his harmonica in the middle of a busy shopping mall. Striding over, a policeman asked, "May I please see your permit?"

"I don't have one," Dunwiddy confessed.

"In that case, you'll have to accompany me."

"Splendid!" Dunwiddy exclaimed. "What shall we sing?"

2. Not everyone in the mall was a music hater, however. When a violinist showed up one afternoon, many people stopped and listened to the plaintive melodies he nursed from his instrument. One particularly lovely tune moved Mrs. Phelps to tears.

Placing a twenty-dollar bill in the musician's open case, she said, "That was the most beautiful song I've ever heard."

"Thank you. I wrote it for my dear, departed wife. Unfortunately, it never sold."

"Really?" Mrs. Phelps said. "I'm surprised."

"So was I, especially since everyone who heard it said it was the most romantic tune since the days of Chopin. But they insisted that I change the title."

"Why, that's absurd!" she said. "I don't care what a song is called, it's the melody that matters."

"I agree," replied the musician.

Curious, Mrs. Phelps asked, "What is it called?"

" 'I Love You So Goddamn Much, My Darlin', I Could Shit.' "

3. Alas, the amateur pianist worked at night and was never able to find anyone to accompany

him during the day. Thus he was forced to go out and buy a duet-yourself kit.

4. According to most conductors, whenever Beethoven's Ninth Symphony is on the program, the bass violinists must be selected with extreme care. There's a lengthy stretch during which there are no bass violin parts; at this time the bass section becomes restless and cognac is frequently passed around.

   If this happens, it is the responsibility of the first violinist to inform the conductor, which he or she does by passing a note which reads simply, "Top of the Ninth, basses loaded."

5. And to make matters worse, while the conductor is preoccupied, some wiseacre usually takes a spool of catgut and binds all the music, leaving the score tied. . . .

**MUSSOLINI**  *See also* CASTRO, NICARAGUA, RUSSIA, STALIN

1. After making the trains run on time in Italy, Il Duce was feeling good about himself. Thus he ordered the government printing office to issue a stamp bearing his likeness. Much to his horror, however, postal carriers began complaining that the stamps were falling off envelopes. Every day their bags would be full of them.

Paying a visit on the printer, Mussolini demanded to know why the highest grade of glue hadn't been used on *his* commemorative stamp.

"Oh, but it was," the trembling authority assured him. "We've looked into this unfortunate situation, and the problem, sir, is that people are spitting on the wrong side!"

2. Burning with anger after the fate of his postage stamp, Il Duce decided to forget his troubles by going out. Putting on a false beard and slipping into a slouch hat, he went to the movies.

Shortly after he sat down, the newsreel began. Naturally, his exploits were very much a part of it. However, much to his surprise, when he was seen on the screen, everyone in the theater rose and gave the film a rousing ovation. Overcome, the tyrant remained in his seat.

Suddenly the man standing next to him said, "Pssst! Mister! Most of the people feel as you do, but it would be safer if you stood and clapped!"

3. It wasn't that he was only a bad leader, Mussolini was also a bad military planner. Seems he left his armies high and dry once when they asked for shells and he sent ziti. . . .

4. Eventually, of course, Mussolini passed on.
One day St. Peter visited hell to make cer-

tain that sinners were being adequately punished. During his tour he noticed that Hitler was standing in feces up to his chin. Surprisingly, the Fuhrer was smiling.

"I don't understand," said St. Peter. "How can you smile when you'll be spending all of eternity in excrement?"

Hitler replied, "I'm smiling because I'm standing on Mussolini's shoulders."

5. After centuries of this unpleasantness, Mussolini was allowed to petition heaven for admittance. Though he was covered with filth, he was so anxious to get out of hell that he didn't bother to wash. He just hurried to his audience with St. Peter.

The guardian of the pearly gates looked him over. "Before I can interview you, you must prove to me that you are, in fact, Mussolini."

Despite all that was at stake, the arrogant tyrant shouted, "Prove it! How dare you ask *me* such a thing."

"Look," St. Peter said, "Shakespeare had to identify himself, Chopin did too, and so did Van Gogh, Victor Hugo, and Michelangelo."

"Who the hell are they?" the shit-covered man demanded.

Frowning, St. Peter said, "Have a seat. You're Mussolini, all right."

## NATURAL DISASTERS

1. The residents of a small Pennsylvania village woke up one morning as the river overflowed and flood waters literally rose to the rooftops.

   Sitting atop their chimney, two little boys were surveying the scene. Cars floated by, a doghouse and a dog drifted past, and suddenly one of them noticed a beret moving first one way in the water, then the other.

   "Hey," said one boy, "do you see that hat? First it goes this way, then that way, then back again."

   "Oh," answered the other, "that's my dad. Last night he said that come hell or high water, he was going to mow the lawn today."

## NERDS

1. Q: What happened when the nerd with a hard-on ran into a wall?
   A: He broke his nose.

## NICARAGUA                    *See also* CASTRO, RUSSIA 7

1. Addressing his people, Daniel Ortega said, "My countrymen: When I took over this country, our economy was poised on the edge of an

abyss. Well, I am proud to announce that since then, we have taken a step forward. . . ."

2. Q: Why did Ortega jail the rebel orchestra?
   A: He maintained that any contraband is illegal.

3. Assigned to report on war-torn Nicaragua for a news service, a journalist returned to the country he had covered a decade before. As fate would have it, while he was driving through the countryside where contras and government forces had been known to clash, he encountered a peasant couple he had met ten years before. He recalled distinctly that then the man had been out walking with his son, his wife walking some distance behind. Today the positions were reversed.

   Sensing a story in the improved status of women, the reporter went over and asked what had happened.

   "Has the tradition changed?" he asked. "Is it social progress?"

   "No," the man replied. "It's land mines."

4. While patrolling the jungles outside Managua, government soldiers captured a rebel sniper.

   While the captive was being bound, he snarled, "We contras fight for our honor, while you fight only for pay!"

   Snorting, the government soldier said, "Why not? Each of us fights for what we don't have."

## NICKNAMES

1. Filling out a job application, Bernie Wyzinski followed the instructions to the letter. Where it said NAME, he filled in, "Wyzinski, Bernie." And where it said NICKNAME, he wrote, "Hole, ass."

2. Then there was the sex-hungry young grocery clerk who was referred to by the men at the store as Frito Lay. . . .

## NOAH'S ARK

1. During religious classes, Mrs. Pritchett asked little Val to name the first person who came off the ark after the flood. He was unable to answer, and the teacher said, "Why, it was Noah."

   Scowling, Val flipped open his Bible and said, "Uh-uh."

   "What do you mean?" the teacher asked.

   Val replied, "It says right here that Noah came forth. . . ."

2. Alas, there wasn't much to do on the ark. Seems they couldn't even play cards, because of the hippos standing on the deck. . . .

3. When the waters finally subsided, however, and Noah led all the animals onto dry land, he

was distraught by a pair of snakes which refused to leave.

Arms on his hips, he glared down at them. "So? Why won't you leave?"

"Because we can't do what the Lord has asked," replied one of the snakes.

"You mean you can't go forth and multiply? Why not?"

The snake said sadly, "Because we're adders."

## NUCLEAR ACCIDENTS

1. Q: What are the Russians doing with the Chernobyl nuclear power plant?
   A: They're transforming it into a synagogue.

2. Then there was the physicist who caused a catastrophe at the nuclear research facility. Seems he had too many ions in the fire. . . .

3. Q: What do you get from consuming Ukrainian dairy products?
   A: The Trotskis.

4. Q: How many Ukrainians does it take to screw in a light bulb?
   A: None. When Ukrainians are around, you don't need light bulbs.

5. Then there's the new soup produced in Kiev: Leek.

6. Which is not quite as deadly as the new element Soviet scientists have discovered: Ukranium.

**NUDISTS**     *See also* LADY GODIVA, ADAM AND EVE 7

1. Q: Why did the young woman go to the nude beach?
   A: To snatch a few rays.

**NUMBERS**     *See also* SCHOOL 2

1. Q: If two's company and three's a crowd, what are four and five?
   A: Nine.

2. It was the first day of school, and the first grade teacher decided to see how much her students knew about math.

   "Mickey, can you tell me what is 3 and 2?"

   Mickey said, "That's when you should watch very, very carefully before you swing at the next pitch."

1. Q: On what day is a nymphomaniac forced to
   make the toughest decision of her life?
   A: The day she meets a guy who has a fourteen-
   inch dick . . . and herpes.

2. When the man asked his widower father why
   he'd married a young nymphomaniac whom
   he could never satisfy instead of a woman his
   own age, the old man said, "Son, I'd rather
   have ten percent of a good business than a
   hundred percent interest in a bankrupt one."

3. Comparing notes, one Southern woman said
   to the other, "Horny men are all alike."
       Nodding, the other Southern belle said,
   "Horny men are all Ah like, too."

4. "Doctor," said the sex-crazed young lass, "what
   ever can I do? I absolutely *hate* myself when I
   get up in the morning."
       Stroking his beard, the doctor said, "In that
   case, I suggest you sleep until noon."

5. Q: How can you tell when a biology student
   is a nymphomaniac?
   A: Instead of dissecting grasshoppers, she's
   busy opening flies.

6. Then there was the sex-starved young ms. who simply hated being stood up.

7. . . . and the nymphomaniac who couldn't stop laughing. She'd walk around all day going, "He, he, he!"

8. . . . or the man-hungry young woman who had only one complaint about sex on TV: she kept falling off.

9. And finally, there was the nymphomaniac who took an office job, hoping to find sexual harassment.


## OPTOMETRISTS
See also ART 1

1. Feeling his way into the optometrist's office, Jake said, "I sat on my eyeglasses and busted them. Will the doctor have to examine me all over again?"

   "No," said the receptionist. "Just your eyes.'


## ORGASMS
See also SEX, JEWISH AMERICAN PRINCESSES 7

1. Naturally, only the Japanese would define an orgasm as a gland finale. . . .

1. "Sir," said the panhandler to a man in the street, "can you spare ten dollars?"

   "Ten dollars!" exclaimed the man. "What makes you think you can ask people for money like that?"

   "I just thought," replied the beggar, "that it'd be best to put all my begs in one ask it."

2. With a hat in each hand, the beggar approached a woman walking down the street. "Ma'am," he said, "can I have a few dollars?"

   "Fine," she said, reaching into her purse, "but why do you have two hats?"

   "Well, business has been so good that I decided to open a branch office."

3. "Excuse me," the beggar said to a store owner, "but I haven't eaten in days. Can I have a penny?"

   "A penny? What can you do with that?"

   The beggar replied, "I'm very anxious to weigh myself."

4. The beggar walked up to a man and said, "Sir, would you let me have a hundred dollars for a cup of coffee?"

   "One hundred dollars!" screamed the man. "My good fellow, that is ridiculous!"

Growing indignant, the beggar said, "Give me a yes or no, fella, but don't tell me how to run my business!"

## PARTIES

See also EGOTISTS 5, GAMES 1

1. On the occasion of their fiftieth wedding anniversary, Mr. Bell decided to forego a big party and treat Mrs. Bell to a memorable evening at home. Quietly filling the bathtub with champagne, he called her into the bathroom and they spent a delightful evening together.

   When they were finished, Mr. Bell was disinclined to waste the champagne. Thus he carefully poured it back into the empty bottles. However, when he was finished, he found he had nearly a half-bottle too much.

   Frowning, he said, "Oh, darling, you didn't!"

2. After riffling through the local directory, a woman found the number she was looking for and dialed.

   "Game warden," said the voice on the other end.

   "Oh, good!" the woman said, "I'd appreciate it if you'd give me some suggestions for my little boy's party."

3. Upon leaving the dull cocktail party, one couple was overheard to comment that it was a fete worse than death. . . .

220

## PEDIATRICIANS *See also* DOCTORS

1. Dr. Marks, the pediatrician, was a man known to have very little patients. . . .

## PHILOSOPHERS

1. It was a violent storm, but Rene Descartes and his colleague Raoul had agreed to attend a philosopher's convention in Paris. En route, their carriage became hopelessly mired in the mud. Refusing to accept defeat, Descartes leapt from the carriage, pushed the driver aside, and began pulling on the horse. The animal bolted and knocked the philosopher back into the mud.

   Raoul climbed out and they helped the dazed Frenchman to his feet. "In the future," the driver said to Raoul, "you would be wise not to put Descartes before the horse."

2. The eminent Chinese writer and philosopher was touring the U.S., giving lectures on college campuses. At one stop, after lightning struck the auditorium, all the lights went out. The sponsor of the gathering hurriedly collected all the spare bulbs in the building, handed them out to the audience, and had the old ones replaced.

   When the hall was again illuminated, the

writer smiled and said, "You have all shown the truth of the ancient proverb, 'Many hands make light work.' "

## PIGS

1. The ten unusually small pigs walked into the bar and ordered beer after beer. As the night progressed, all but one of them made at least a dozen trips to the bathroom.

   After the bartender brought him his twentieth brew, he asked the one pig, "Say, how come you've been drinking all night, yet you haven't gone to the john once?"

   The pig looked up. "Because I'm the one that goes wee-wee-wee-wee-wee all the way home."

2. Young Phil came calling for his farmer friend Zebulon.

   "I can't come out to play," said Zeb.

   "Why?"

   "Cause I was out in the barn, screwing the pig, and my dad caught me."

   "Idiot!" said Phil. "You're only supposed to do that when it's dark."

   "It was!"

   "Then how'd your dad find out?"

   Zeb replied, "The pig squealed."

1. "Doc," said the old woman, "my left foot is killing me."

    "I'm afraid there isn't much we can do," he said. "It's simply old age."

    "Old age, old shmage," she shot back. "My right foot is fine, and it's just as old!"

2. Looking for a brothel, a drunk walked into a podiatrist's office by accident. Winking at the receptionist, he said, "Ya know what I'm here for!"

    She said she did, and told him to go into the doctor's office, sit on the examining table, and place his extremity on the extension.

    The drunk did as he was told, unzipping his fly and laying his member on the cushion. When the nurse walked in, she yelled, "Hey! That's not a foot!"

    Frowning, the drunk said, "Since when is there a minimum?"

**THE POLICE**          *See also* DRUNKS 2, ELEPHANTS 1,
JEWS 1, MOTHERS-IN-LAW 2,
MUSIC 1, RUSSIANS 2, 18

1. Stepping out of his rural church, Father Schulkind was surprised to find several large dead pigs in the garden. Realizing they must

have escaped from a local farm, he telephoned the police to come and take the animals away.

"Gee, father," said the smart-aleck desk sergeant, "I don't think we can make it. I mean, isn't it the job of the church to bury the dead?"

"Quite so," replied the quick-thinking priest. "However, it's also our responsibility to notify the next-of-kin."

*THE POLISH*          *See also* AIRPLANES 3, BIOLOGY 1,
CHRISTMAS 1, CIRCUS 2, COWS 2,
CRIME 4, 5, EXECUTIONS 1, 2, FARMERS 2,
FOOTBALL 11, 14, GENITALS 1, HUNTERS 5,
INVENTIONS 1, 3, LAVATORIES 3, NICKNAMES 1,
PROSTITUTES 11, RUSSIANS 23, SKYDIVING 3,
TERRORISTS 2, WORLD WAR II 1, 3

1. An American couple, a French couple, and a Polish couple were dining out. The American man said to his date, "Would you please pass me the sugar, sweetie?"

   Smiling at his own companion, the Frenchman said, "Would you pass me the honey, honey?"

   Looking to be as suave as the other men, the Pole said to his girlfriend, "Would you please pass me the milk, cow?"

2. Q: What happened to the Pole when he learned he'd been promoted from the third grade to the fourth?
   A: He was so excited, he cut himself while shaving.

3. The Pole attended the board of finance meeting, spoiling for a fight. He wasn't disappointed.

"It's decided, then," said the chairperson. "The budget surplus will be divided as follows: $9,000 will go to education, and $1,000 will go to the high school bowling team."

Shooting to his feet, the Pole protested, "I don't see why in hell we have to give half the money to education!"

4. Abramowicz walked into the shop and ordered a pound of kielbasa. The clerk behind the counter looked at him strangely.

"What's wrong?" Abramowicz snapped. "Are you thinking, 'The guy ordered kielbasa, so he must be Polish. And if he's Polish, he must be a moron?' "

"No, sir—"

"If someone walked in and ordered corned beef, would you say, 'There's an Irishman. He must be a drunk?' "

"No, sir—"

"Or if a person walked in and ordered grits, would you say, 'There's a Southerner. He must be a redneck.' "

"No, sir."

"Then what *is* it?"

"Sir, this is a hardware store."

5. Q: What do the numbers 1942 and 2001 have in common?

A: They're adjoining rooms at the Warsaw Sheraton.

6. The Polish couple loved the drive-in, but froze to death when they made the mistake of going to see *Closed for Winter*.

7. More fortunate, though not much brighter, was the young Polish couple which hated the film at the drive-in, grew rowdy, and ripped up the seats.

8. While driving through the back roads of a little town, the Polish truckers came to an overpass with a sign which read, "CLEARANCE: 11'3"." They got out and measured their rig, which was 12'4" tall.

   "What do you think?" said one as they climbed back into the cab.

   The driver looked around conspiratorially, then shifted into first. "Not a cop in sight. Let's take a chance!"

9. Driving on, the Poles get a flat tire. Climbing out to change it, one trucker says to the other, "Damn! I'll bet it was the fork in the road that did it!"

10. Wanting to pursue a career that would test his courage to the utmost, the young Pole passed up the marines, and decided not to be a police officer, in order to become a peanut vendor.

This, just because he overheard someone say that all those guys do day after day is whistle while their nuts burn.

11. During the summit of communist leaders, the rulers of Russia, China, and Poland were strolling along a beach on the Black Sea. Things hadn't been going well; the break had been called because the Soviet and Chinese delegations were at each others' throats. The Polish delegation presented no problem, being forced to support the Russian line.

While walking in tense silence, the Russian leader spotted a strange, ornate object poking from the beach. Retrieving it, he began brushing off the sand; suddenly a huge genie appeared before the rulers.

In a great voice he said, "To each of you I grant a single wish."

"You mean," said the Pole, "we can ask for anything we want?"

"That's correct," said the djinn.

Speaking first, the Russian said, "I wish that the entire Chinese would see things *my* way."

Chuckling, the Chinese ruler said, "I wish that the entire Russian delegation would see things *my* way!"

Squinting toward the bright blue sky, the Pole said, "I wish I had some suntan lotion."

12. Q: How did the boss know he'd hired a Polish secretary?

A: There was White-out all over the computer screen.

13. It took awhile, but the Polish mother finally taught her son to put on a new pair of underwear every day. Unfortunately, by the end of the week he couldn't pull his trousers on. . . .

14. After giving a lecture in which he cracked several Polish jokes, the self-help instructor was cornered by one of the members of the audience.

    "My name is Jill Opaszinski, and I was wondering: do you read Polish?"

    "No," said the man, "I don't."

    "Do you speak it?"

    "No, can't say that I do."

    "Then I wonder," Jill said, "how does it feel to be dumber than one of us Polacks?"

15. Q: Why did the Polish track team train with their Walkmans on?
    A: Because the tape went, "Left, right, left, right, left. . . ."

16. During the First World War, a German and three Polish pilots got into a vicious dogfight. The German was able to shoot down two of the Poles before the third riddled his plane with bullets and sent him into a tailspin.

    The pilot was badly mangled but survived, and found himself in a Polish hospital. Visited by the pilot who had shot him down, he said, "T-tonight they're going to amputate my foot. Please, take it up with you next time and drop it over my airfield so my comrades will know what has happened to me."

The Pole agreed and the next morning he did as the German asked. That afternoon he visited the German once again.

"T-tonight," the German said, "they're going to amputate my other foot. I implore you, as a fellow pilot—please drop it over my airfield as a salute to my brave comrades."

The following day the Pole once more did as the German asked. That afternoon he visited the pilot again.

"T-tonight," said the German, "my right arm is going to be amputated. Can I impose upon you to drop it over my airfield as you did my two feet?"

His eyes narrowing, the Pole said, "Now just a minute, is this for real, or are you trying to escape?"

17. While traveling in Ireland, an American, a Frenchman, and a Pole learned of a magic cliff. According to villagers, if you have the courage to leap from the cliff, then you shall become whatever you scream on the way down.

Locating the enchanted bluff, the trio climbed to the top. The American screwed up his courage, leaped, and shouted, "Billionaire!"

Suddenly a private jet swooped down and spirited him away.

Encouraged, the Frenchman ran from the cliff and shouted, "Eagle!" and was transformed into a majestic bird. Rubbing his hands together, the Pole ran for the cliff. Unfortunately, he tripped over a rock and fell from the precipice, screaming, "Oh, shit!"

18. As part of its duties as a Warsaw Pact nation, Poland was obliged to supply a naval destroyer for maneuvers in the Black Sea. Needless to say, the Russian sponsors were rather distressed when Admiral Mankewicz showed up carrying a hula hoop with a nail hammered through it. . . .

19. Then there was the Pole who moved from Warsaw to Little Rock, Arkansas, and raised the IQ of both cities.


**POLITICIANS**     *See also* DIPLOMATS, PRESIDENTS,
CANNIBALS 2, DISEASES 3, GOD 4, SODOMY 3

1. Arriving in Los Angeles for campaigning, the presidential candidate checked into one of the poshest hotels in town. Upon being shown to his room, he found a voluptuous young woman lying naked in the bed.

   Turning to the bellhop, he said, "What's the meaning of this? Are you trying to cause a *scandal*? I'm going to be the next president of the United States, and your establishment has the *nerve* to insult and offend me in this manner? I intend to sue the management for every penny it has!"

While the bellhop was quaking beneath the verbal onslaught, the sexy young miss quietly slid from the bed and began dressing. Noticing what she was doing, the candidate turned and said, "Hold on, young lady. No one's talking to you."

2. "Have you ever noticed," the NASA mathematician asked a colleague, "that government is the only place where problems are multiplied by divisions?"

3. Two philosophers were sitting at a restaurant, discussing whether or not there was a difference between misfortune and disaster.

"There is most certainly a difference," said one. "If the cook suddenly died and we couldn't have our dinner, that would be a misfortune—but certainly not a disaster. On the other hand, if a cruise ship carrying the Congress were to sink in the middle of the ocean, that would be a disaster—but by no stretch of the imagination would it be a misfortune."

4. Every week the teacher asked her fifth-grade students to use different words in sentences.

This week she gave little Victor the word "Republicans."

"My cat just had a litter," he said, "and all the kittens are Republicans."

"That's very creative," said the teacher.

The following week she called on Victor again and asked him to use the word "Democrats."

"My cat just had a litter," he said, "and all the kittens are Democrats."

The teacher said, "Now, Victor, don't you think you ought to use a different sentence?"

"It *is* different," he replied. "They've opened their eyes now."

5. During a whistle-stop campaign, the presidential candidate's train hopped the track and ran roughshod through a farmer's field. Several animals were killed and the politician agreed to reimburse him, making it the first and only time a politician took responsibility for the bulls hit.

6. It was a Memorial Day celebration, and the senator used the occasion to announce, "I am going to go to the presidential convention and run as a favorite son."

Listening to the speech, one man said to another, "Did I miss somethin', or did that jerk forget to finish the sentence?"

7. In 1984 Walter Mondale asked Gary Hart, "Where's the Beef?" In 1987 Hart provided the answer: it's in the Rice.

8. Then there was one politician's idea of safe sex: no press.

9. Q: What's the opposite of progress?
   A: Congress.

10. Q: What's the difference between Moses and a politician?
    A: Moses' was a voice crying in the wilderness. A politician's voice cries from one.

11. Then there was the newspaper editorial which took to describing the mayoral candidate as a foghorn. "Not only is he bombastic," wrote the paper, "but his biggest failing is that he repeatedly calls attention to a problem without ever doing a thing about it."

## PORNOGRAPHY

See also EXHIBITIONISTS, SEX, VOYEURS

1. As a prerequisite for his job with a very conservative corporation, a young man was sent for a psychiatric evaluation. Picking up a stack of cards, the doctor showed the patient a pair of parallel lines. "When you look at this, what do you see?"

"Two people making love," he answered.

The doctor held up a picture showing a rectangle. "What does this remind you of?"

"A penis."

"And this?" the doctor asked as he held up a triangle.

"A pussy."

The psychiatrist laid down the cards. "I'm afraid I can't recommend you for the job, young man. All you think about is sex."

"Me?" the man yelled. "Who's the guy with the collection of dirty pictures?"

## THE POST OFFICE

See also HOMOSEXUALS 4, MUSSOLINI 1

1. The new clerk was sent to the post office by his boss to mail a rather large envelope. When he reached the window, the woman behind the counter weighed it.

   "I'm sorry," she said, "but this is too heavy. You need to put more stamps on it."

   "Idiot!" the customer yelled. "That'll only make it *heavier!*"

2. When office assistant Casper came back from lunch, his boss asked, "Did you mail that very important envelope I gave you?"

   "Yes, Mr. Drake," said the youth. Beaming, he handed his employer a fistful of change.

   "What's this?"

"The money you gave me for the stamps."
He whispered conspiratorily, "I slipped the
envelope into the box when no one was
looking."

3. Then there was the small Chinese island which
finally got mail service, the carrier coming
over by boat. Naturally, all they got was junk
mail.

## POVERTY                    *See also* PANHANDLERS

1. Sitting down heavily on the barstool, Parker
said to the bartender, "Gimme a whiskey. I'm
gonna need it—gonna be a big fight."

After the drink was poured, Parker downed
it and ordered a second. When he was finished, he dragged his sleeve across his mouth,
ordered a third, and turned into the bar.

"Hey!" he shouted. "Anyone here a doctor?" A man replied in the affirmative, and as
he swallowed the third drink, Parker said,
"Stay put. Yer gonna have yer work cut out for
ya."

Parker ordered a fourth shot, then turned
back into the room. "Anybody here an under-
taker?" Someone admitted that he was, and,
gulping down the whiskey, Parker said, "Good.
You're gonna be needed."

Swinging back to the bar, Parker asked for
another drink.

"Man," said the bartender, "you weren't kidding. This is gonna be *some* fight."

"You bet."

"Who's it going to be with?" he asked, pouring the drink.

Parker drained the glass and slammed it on the bar. "You, pal. I ain't got a dime to my name."

## PREGNANCY

See also SEX, SPERM BANKS, ACCENTS 7, ESKIMOS 3

1. Dinah met her friend Patrice on the Watts street corner.

   "Didja hear?" Dinah said. "Young Virginia's gettin' married?"

   "Married?" said Patrice. "I didn't even know she was pregnant!"

2. Q: What's the difference between a light bulb and a pregnant woman?

   A: The light bulb can be unscrewed.

3. The gynecologist walked into the examining room, a smile on his lips.

   "Helen, you can go home and tell your husband the good news: you're going to have a baby."

   Helen said, "But, doctor, I'm not married."

   "Oh. In that case, go home and tell your boyfriend."

236

Helen said, "But, doctor, I haven't got a boyfriend."

The doctor scratched his head. "In that case, go home and tell your parents to prepare for the Second Coming."

**PREJUDICE**        *See also* BLACKS, MEXICANS, JOKES 1, THE POLISH 14

1. Of course, there's nothing lower than the hypocrite who doesn't mind screwing a black girl, but doesn't want his kids to go to school with her.

2. While Mr. and Mrs. Zachary were walking down the street, Mr. Zachary paused to give the monkey a dollar.

   "I'm surprised at you," Mrs. Zachary said when they walked on. "You *hate* gypsies."

   "I know," he said, "but they're irresistible when they're little."

3. St. Peter was busy interviewing the dead to determine which ones deserve a place in heaven.

   "Name?" he asked a black man.

   "Walt Lee."

   "Town of death?"

   "Oopala, Mississippi."

   "Is there any particular act of bravery or kindness which entitles you to pass through the pearly gates?"

"Well," he said, "I was the first black man in Oopala to marry a white woman."

"I see. And when did you do that?"

Walt answered, "About four minutes ago."

4. Q: When does a Spik become a Spaniard?
   A: When he marries your daughter.

5. Touring South Africa with the country's foreign minister, United Nations observer Pierre Girard ordered his driver to stop on the beach. Getting out, the Frenchman looked toward the ocean, where there were two white men in a motor boat; behind them, a black man was waterskiing.

   "Well," said M. Girard, smiling, "there's something I shall be happy to report back to the human rights commission."

   While the observer returned to the car, the foreign minister stood a moment with the driver.

   "Well," said the government official, "it's clear that M. Girard knows little about shark patrols."

6. While O'Quinn lay on his deathbed, barely clinging to life, he sent for his pastor. Wheezing horribly, he indicated that he wished to renounce his Catholic faith and become a Protestant.

   "But why, man!" the clergyman exclaimed.

"Because," said O'Quinn, "if someone's got t'die, then let it be one o' *them* bastards!"

7. Two Mexicans strolled into a bar in Texas. No sooner had they sat down than a pair of brawny Texans ambled over.

"We don't like yer kind here," one of the Texans drawled. "How about you step outside?"

Seeing as how all eyes were upon them, the Mexicans reluctantly obliged. Two minutes later, they walked back in and sat down at the bar.

"Jeez," said the bartender, filling their order, "what happened out there?"

"As soon as we walked out," said one, "those gringos went for their razors."

"Really!"

"It wasn't a problem, though," said the other. "They had no place to plug them."

8. After just two days of driving through Mexico, Steve was sick and tired of Mexicans. "They hate Americans," he told his wife, "and I swear to God—the next one I see, I'm going to make that son of a bitch suffer!"

As it happened, Steve's anger was such that he didn't look where he was going, and rear-ended a brawny farmer in a pickup truck. The Mexican came over and leaned in Steve's window.

"Hey, greengo—why did you heet my truck?"

"Because I can't stand you or any other

Mexican greaseballs!" Steve ranted. "In fact, if you're man enough, I'm going to come out and kick the shit out of you!"

The Mexican motioned Steve out. "I make a deal weet you," he said. "If you ween, you take my truck. If I ween, not only do I fuck your wife, but you weel hold my balls to keep them off the hot street."

The men agreed and fought. Later, Steve was smiling as he and his wife drove off.

"I told you'd I'd make some Mexican suffer!" he gloated.

His wife looked at him. "What the *hell* are you talking about?"

Steve smiled. "Didn't you hear how he screamed when I dropped his balls on the asphalt?"

9. Q: What's a nigger?
   A: A black who has just left the room.

10. Rhett, a Southern gentleman, was none too thrilled when his daughter Lil came home from college with Rupert, a black man. Still, Rhett was delighted to see his little girl, and threw a party for her. The bash was held on the shores of their private lake.

    After drinking a great deal, Rhett announced that the lake was filled with piranhas, and that whoever swam across it could have his daughter's hand in marriage.

    Though there were many eligible bachelors

at the shindig, none jumped in. Finally there was a mighty splash, and Rupert's arms and legs were churning madly as he raced across the lake.

Smiling gleefully, Lil raced to the opposite shore, where she helped Rupert from the waters.

"Oh darlin'!" she yelled, hugging him, "I'm yours! I'm yours!"

Looking back, Rupert snarled, "I don't want *you*. I want the son of a bitch that pushed me *in*!"

11. When the Chinese delivery boy dropped off Goldberg's lunch, the World War II vet looked up from his desk and socked the boy.

"Why'd you do that?"

"That's for Pearl Harbor!" Goldberg cried.

Rubbing his chin, the boy said, "But I'm not Japanese! I'm Vietnamese!"

"Chinese, Vietnamese, Japanese—they're all the same to me."

Later that day Goldberg was walking down the street when the delivery boy rammed into him with his bicycle. Sprawled on the street, Goldberg snarled, "Why'd you do that?"

"That's for the *Titanic*!" the boy yelled.

"The *Titanic*? I didn't have anything to do with that!"

"Goldberg, Blumberg, Iceberg—they're all the same to me!"

12. Two men were sitting on the park bench, Sol reading the newspaper.

"I see here," he says to the stranger, "that the Israelis arrested five terrorists trying to hijack a plane."

"To hell with the Israelis," the other man said.

"Why?" said Sol. "Look at all they've done! Under Ben-Gurion, they turned a desert into a habitable land!"

"To hell with Ben-Gurion."

"What? How can you say that? What about the way Moshe Dayan led them to victory in—"

"To hell with Moshe Dayan," the man barked.

"Say," said Sol, looking the man over, "just what nationality are you, anyway?"

"Irish," the man said proudly.

Rising, Sol threw back his shoulders and said, "Then to hell with Ella Fitzgerald!"

## PRESIDENTS

See also THE DEFICIT, POLITICIANS, GENEALOGY 1

1. Former presidents Nixon and Ford and candidate Gary Hart were guests on a political-issues cruise. Suddenly, while they were in the midst of a panel discussion, the ship sprung a leak. As it began to sink, President Ford said, "Let's help get the women to the lifeboats!"

Nixon ran toward a lifeboat, howling, "Screw the women!"

Glancing at the rising waterline, Hart asked, "Do you think there's time?"

2. Q: How do most Americans feel about the way the Reagan administration has handled the nation's economy?

   A: They couldn't be more indebted.

3. Q: What makes former President Nixon think the country is beginning to forget all about his numerous infractions?

   A: When people wave at him now, some actually use all five fingers.

## PRISON

*See also* CRIME, POLICE, FISH 2, RUSSIANS 14

1. Interviewing the convict after the publication of his first book, the reporter asked, "Why did you decide to list the author as '06801?' "

   "What else would I use?" the prisoner said. "That's my pen name?"

2. Trying to make conversation, one criminal said to the other, "I suppose you're going to have a hot time when you're through with this place."

   "I expect so," said the seasoned felon. "I'm in for life."

3. Then there was the small-town sheriff who nicknamed his jail "Amoeba" because it only had one cell.

## PROGRESS

1. It's an odd fact: science has enabled manufacturers to produce a sixty-cent soft drink which will last for decades, but a $20,000 car still rots in just five years.

2. Progress, of course, is a double-edged sword: it takes shorter and shorter to get to Europe, but longer and longer to get to work.

3. Of all the women in the marketplace at the turn of the century, the most admirable was the first switchboard operator. She hated her job, but she kept plugging away at it.

4. In 1920, when the market for horseshoes began to dwindle, the ambitious blacksmith turned to manufacturing cast-iron toilets. He was proud to be known as a man who was always forging ahead.

5. After years of research in producing better foods, the Future Fruit Company merged with Agricultural Tomorrows, and made a perfect pear.

## PROPOSALS

*See also* DATING,
ENGAGEMENTS, MARRIAGE

1. Alice frowned at the man who, crouched on one knee, was proposing to her.

   "I'm sorry, Jack," she said. "I just can't marry you."

   "Why?" he asked. "Is there someone else?"

   The frown deepened. "Oh, Jack . . . there *must* be."

2. Q: How do young men propose in Harlem?
   A: "You're going to have a *what*?"

## PROSTITUTES

*See also* SEX, BIRDS 2,
CARTOON CHARACTERS 2, ELEPHANTS 3,
ESKIMOS 1, 2, 3, PODIATRISTS 2,
SADISTS 2, SENIOR CITIZENS 2, TOURISTS 5,
VENEREAL DISEASES 3, VOYEURS 2

1. Fearing that she might be a hemophiliac, the prostitute went to see her doctor.

   "It's awful," she says. "Every time I get even a small cut, it takes days for the bleeding to stop."

   "I see," said the physician. "And how much do you lose when you get your period?"

   She thought for a moment, then answered, "About a grand."

2. "Had the strangest sexual encounter of my life last night," Bill said to Frank. "A blind call girl."

"Really?" said Frank.

"Yeah. You gotta hand it to her."

3. Q: What's the difference between a cheap hooker and an elephant?

A: One lies on its back for peanuts. The other lives at the zoo.

4. Q: What do a streetwalker and a deer have in common?

A: They both do it for bucks.

5. Then there was the male hustler who took pleasure in referring to himself as a fee-male.

6. Q: What do you call a prostitute from Montreal?

A: A Canadian Mountee.

7. Sitting at the bar, one real estate agent complained to another, "Christ, man, if I don't sell more homes this month, I'm gonna lose my goddam ass." Happening to glance to one side, he noticed an attractive young woman sitting two stools away. "Sorry," he said quickly. "I wouldn't have spoken like that if I'd known you were there."

"That's all right," she said. "Hell, if I don't sell more ass this month, I'm going to lose my goddam home."

8. It was an unusually busy night at the whore-house, though not quite a sellout. Thus the madam went ahead and put a sign on the door: LAST BUTT NOT LEASED.

9. The reason that "butt" was available was because she was an intellectual whore who would only LXIX her customers.

10. Doubling over with pain, the prostitute is rushed to the hospital and given an appendectomy. Unfortunately, the doctor sews up the wrong hole, thus forcing the whore to make all her money on the side.

11. "Hey," the hooker said to the passing Pole, "what can you do about my itchy pussy."
    "Nothing," said the man. "I don't know diddly about Japanese cars."

12. Then there was the pimp who wanted to improve his image and insisted on being called a fornicaterer. . . .

13. In our previous tome we told you about the whorehouse sign which read, "OUT TO LUNCH. GO FUCK YOURSELF." Unfortunately, a lot of the madam's customers thought that was too crude, so she changed it. The sign now reads, "OUT TO LUNCH. BEAT IT!"

1. While walking to the ninth hole, one psychiatrist said to the other, "Would you believe that yesterday I had a patient who claimed he heard music every time he put on his hat?"

   "Really? What did you do?"

   The psychiatrist answered, "I took it away and removed the band."

2. "I give up," Natalie said to her girlfriend over lunch. "I'm going to quit my job."

   "I thought you always wanted to work for a psychiatrist," her friend said.

   "I did, but I can't win with him. When I'm early for work, he says I have an anxiety complex. When I'm late, he tells me I'm being hostile. And when I'm on time, he says I'm being compulsive."

3. Lying down in the couch, Mr. Caldwell said to his psychiatrist, "You've got to do something. Last night I dreamed I was in a room with a blonde, a brunette, and a redhead."

   "I don't understand," said the analyst. "What's wrong with that?"

   Mr. Caldwell said, "I dreamt I was also a woman!"

4. Going to see her shrink, Gwen said, "You have to do something! Every time I go on a date, I always end up doing all kinds of perverted sexual acts. And then I spend the next day feeling guilty."

"I understand," said the doctor. "We'll work on improving your willpower."

"No!" she declared. "I want you to work on getting rid of the guilt!"

5. The spinster was feeling extremely tense, so she went to see Dr. Freudlich. The analyst concluded that she was suffering from repressed sexual desires, and hypnotized her in an effort to relieve the problem.

The first thing he did after she was in a trance was ask her to spell "bedroom."

Staring ahead, the young woman said, "B . . . E . . . D . . . R . . . Oh . . . Ohhhh . . . Mmmmmmmmmm."

She left, her stress gone.

6. Looking tired and disgusted, Mr. Lee went to see his doctor. The physician could barely contain his surprise when he saw carrots growing from the man's nostrils.

"My goodness," the doctor said, "no wonder you're upset!"

"You're not kidding," Mr. Lee said. "I planted tomatoes."

7. Dressed as Napoleon, Oscar Weiner went to see a psychiatrist.

"So," the doctor said, "what seems to be the problem?"

"It's terrible," said Mr. Weiner. "I have the most powerful armed forces in Europe, a vast fortune, and the most opulent homes one could want."

"Then what's wrong?"

"It's my wife," said the man. "She thinks she's someone named Mrs. Weiner."

8. When Mr. Goodman arrived at the psychiatrist's office and admitted he hadn't dreamt the night before, the doctor was openly annoyed.

"How am I supposed to help you," he asked, "if you don't do your homework?"

9. Worried when men stopped calling her for dates, the overweight young woman went to see her shrink.

"Why don't you diet?" the psychiatrist suggested.

The young woman thought for a moment. "That's a thought. What color?"

10. Sitting down on the psychiatrist's couch, Mr. Harryhausen began plugging pipe tobacco up his nose.

"Ah," said the doctor, "I'm glad you came. I believe I can help you."

"I believe you can at that," said Mr. Harryhausen. "Have you got a light?"

11. Then there's the analyst who maintains that he doesn't have to worry as long as other people do.

12. "Doctor!" the young woman wailed to her psychiatrist, "I just don't know who else to turn to!"

   "What's the problem?"

   "I can't stop thinking that I'm a box of biscuits!"

   "Oh, really? You mean, those small, square ones?"

   "Yes!"

   "Crisp?"

   "*Yes!*"

   The doctor nodded. "You're definitely crackers."

## RABBITS

See also EASTER 1

1. Q: Why don't rabbits make noise when they mate?
   A: They've got cotton balls.

2. After running over a rabbit, the motorist stopped to try and make its last moments more comfortable. She was joined by a patent medicine man, who happened to be driving by.

   "Y'know," said the man, "I think I may have something t'help this little critter."

   Rushing back to his van, he returned with a

bottle and poured the contents down the furry thing's throat. Suddenly, the animal's ears perked, its nose twitched, and it bounded off.

Amazed, the motorist said, "What on earth did you give that rabbit?"

"What do you think?" said the man. "Hare restorer."

## RACQUETBALL

1. During a ferocious game of racquetball, Oliver was hit so hard with the ball that it lodged itself well up his rectum. He was rushed to the hospital, where there wasn't time to give him more than a local anesthetic before he was rushed into surgery.

   As Oliver lay there, he watched, horrified, as the surgeon cut first in his right side, then in his left, then in his belly, and finally in his chest.

   "Doc!" Oliver cried. "Why are you making so many incisions!"

   "Dammit," the surgeon snapped, "that's just the way the ball bounces!"

## RADON

1. Unfortunately, when guests drop over nowadays, it's usually due to radon. . . .

## REINCARNATION

See also DEATH

1. So convinced was the actress that she'd be coming back after her death, she had herself buried beneath a tombstone which read, "TO BE CONTINUED. . . ."

## RESTAURANTS

*See also* CHEFS, FOOD, AMNESIA 1, EXHIBITIONISTS 2, TEA 1

1. Because the restaurant was located in the heart of the metropolitan theater district, the cashier was always being asked what time it was. Sick and tired of being disturbed while she was adding checks or counting out change, she finally bought a clock and left it on the counter.

   Now as people pay their bills, they no longer ask the time. Instead they say "Is that clock right?"

2. "Waiter," the customer inquired, "why isn't there any soup on the menu?"

   The waiter explained, "I wiped it off."

3. "Waiter!" the customer yelled, looking up from his lunch, "there's a fly in my soup!"

   "Impossible," replied the waiter. "This place is strictly fly-by-night."

4. "Waiter!" snarled the customer, "there's a fly in my soup!"

"You mean, sir," said the waiter, glancing down, "there's soup on your fly."

5. "Waiter!" the customer protested, "there's a fly in my soup!"

The waiter smiled proudly. "Now *there's* a fly who knows good soup."

6. "Waiter!" barked the customer, "there's a fly in my soup!"

"No," the waiter replied, "that's a bee vitamin."

7. "Waiter!" the customer screamed, "there's a fly in my soup!"

"Enjoy him," suggested the waiter, "we've plenty more."

8. "Waiter!" hollered the customer, "there's a fly in my soup!"

"What do you expect for a buck," said the waiter, "a silkworm?"

9. "Waiter!" the customer shrieked, "there's a fly in my soup!"

"Don't worry," the waiter assured him, "the frog will surface any moment now."

10. "Waiter!" wailed the customer, "there's a fly in my soup!"

The waiter frowned. "If you wanted him with the main course, why didn't you *say* so?"

11. "Waiter!" the customer griped, "there are coins in my soup!"

    "Well, sir," said the waiter, "you said you'd stop dining here if there weren't some change in the food."

12. "Waiter!" sneered the customer, "your thumb is in my soup!"

    "Don't worry, sir. It isn't hot."

13. "Waiter," said the impatient customer, "will the hamburger be long?"

    "No sir," replied the waiter. "Round."

14. "Waiter," the customer asked, "how do you serve shrimps?"

    The waiter replied, "We bend down, sir."

15. Then there was the entrepreneur who opened an Afro-French restaurant and called it, "Chez -What?"

## REWARDS

1. Deciding to drive across the country with his prize-winning wirehair fox terrier, the wealthy young man stopped in a small town for a soft drink. When he came out of the country store,

he found that the dog had somehow undone the latch of its cage and bolted through the open window.

After an hour of frantic searching, the man went to the office of the local newspaper. "I'd like to speak with the publisher," he said urgently to a man behind the counter.

"I'm the publisher. What can I do for you?"

The man explained what happened, then said that he wanted to take out an ad.

"Afraid you're out of luck," the publisher said. "This week's edition goes to press in just five minutes."

"Look," the tourist said, "this is a prize-winning, pedigree dog, and I'm offering $2,000 for its safe return!"

Stroking his grizzled chin, the publisher said, "Well . . . if it's that important, you go ahead and write out the ad while I hold the presses."

The man wrote the copy, paid for the ad, then went to a motel to take a room. An hour later, he went back to the newspaper office to pick up a copy of the paper. Not only weren't the presses running, but the publisher and his entire staff were gone. Only a secretary remained.

"Where the hell *is* everyone!" the man yelled. "I thought the presses were ready to roll!"

"Oh, they were," said the woman. "But then the nuttiest thing happened: everyone just ran out to look for someone's lost dog."

2. Attending a lecture at college, a student suddenly realized he'd dropped his wallet. Going to the podium, he said, "Pardon me, but I've lost my wallet with $200 in it. I'll give $25 to anyone who returns it."

From somewhere in the classroom, a voice piped up, "I'll give $50."

## ROCK AND ROLL

See also COUNTRY SINGERS, INDIANS 4

1. After signing autographs for several hours, the rock star said to his manager, "Y'know, I'd give my right arm to be ambidextrous."

2. She'd been a top rock star for years, but then suddenly she insisted on cutting a record of chants. As she put it, she had always wanted to show critics her Bach side.

3. Going backstage, the rock groupie fulfilled a lifelong dream: she kissed every band member in the joint.

4. Then there was the teen who went to the rap concert so he could mangle with the crowd. . . .

1. There came a day when the king fell madly in love with his court jester. More often than not, the potentate could be found at his wit's end.

**RUSSIANS** *See also* CASTRO, MUSSOLINI, NICARAGUA, NUCLEAR ACCIDENTS, STALIN, ADAM AND EVE 6, CANNIBALS 5, COURTROOMS 2, JEWS 1, 6, THE POLISH 11, 18

1. Q: What is the difference between the American Constitution and the Soviet Constitution?
   A: Both guarantee freedom of speech, but only one guarantees freedom afterward as well.

2. After being captured at the border, trying to leave the Soviet Union, the dissident was interrogated by the KGB.

   "Why were you trying to leave?" an officer demanded.

   "Because," said the dissident, "if the government ever fell, my colleagues and I would be blamed."

   "You're a fool!" the man snarled. "The government will never fall!"

   Said the dissident: "Which brings us to my second reason. . . ."

3. While visiting Guyana, the new Soviet foreign minister was introduced to all the members of Guyana's cabinet. He stopped and chuckled when he was presented to the minister of defense.

"Whatever do you do?" the Russian asked. "This is such a tiny country, there is nothing to defend!"

Smiling pleasantly, the minister said, "Sir, I am insulted. When I visited Moscow and was introduced to the minister of justice, I contained *my* laughter."

4. In Moscow a woman went out to do her weekly shopping.

Arriving at the bakery, she found the line reaching well into the next block, so she walked on. At the butcher shop the line was even longer. The same was true at the milk store.

Frustrated beyond words, the woman went to the liquor store to buy a bottle of vodka and relax. There, too, she faced a wait of over two hours.

"I've had enough of this," she muttered and, going home, loaded the pistol her husband had carried during the Second World War. "I'm going to the Kremlin to put an end to the secretary general and his miserable way of running a country!"

Upon arriving, she found three hundred people waiting ahead of her.

5. Allowed to travel to other countries, Vladimir sent postcards to all his friends back in Moscow.

   He wrote from England, "Long live free London! Vladimir."

   He wrote from London, "Long live free Paris! Vladimir."

   Upon returning to the Soviet Union, he wrote, "Long live Moscow! Free Vladimir!"

6. Trying to borrow money from the World Bank, the Soviet finance minister was asked what he could put up for collateral.

   "Well," he said, "we have countless deposits of oil and minerals such as gold and silver."

   "Those are all underground," the agent replied. "What do you have aboveground?"

   Inflating his chest, the minister said, "We have superb Russian leaders."

   Unimpressed, the bank representative said, "You can have your loan, Mr. Minister, when the two trade places."

7. While Gorbachev is giving Daniel Ortega a tour of Moscow, the Nicaraguan leader says, "This is a very nice car. From where does it come?"

   The Soviet ruler replies, "It was made for us by our good friends in Poland."

   "And your suit, sir," Ortega says. "It too is quite elegant."

   Gorbachev says, "It was also given to us by our good friends in Poland."

"Well," Ortega remarks, "they must be very goods friends indeed.'

"Yes," Gorbachev says. "They must."

8. Q: What's the difference between a Russian woman and a Bigfoot?

   A: One is over seven feet tall, smells, and is covered with hair. The other has big feet.

9. Q: Speaking of which, what do you call an attractive woman in Russia?

   A: Tourist.

10. Two government officials were talking about the future of the Soviet Union.

    "Tell me," said one, "what do you think our future will be, three or four years from now?"

    "How should I know?" said the other. "One never knows what our past will be like in three or four years."

11. The Russian teacher stood before the kindergarten class. "In the Soviet Union there is everything," she said. "Plenty of food, good clothing, and nice apartments. And, of course," she said, smiling, "there is always candy for the children to eat."

    As one the children began to chant, "We want to go to the Soviet Union!"

12. Later, the Russian teacher was questioning her young pupils about capitalism and communism.

"What is the goal of United States?" she asked young Caterina.

The girl replied, "The capitalists are trying to find work for the millions whom their system of government has left unemployed, and shelter for the hundreds of thousands who are starving and homeless."

"Now, Nikita," the teacher said, "what is the goal of Soviet Union?"

Nikita replied, "To catch up with U.S.A."

13. Walking into the store, the Russian woman said to the merchant, "So! I see you have no vegetables here!"

"Not true," said the merchant. "We sell bread here, and have no bread. The shop with no vegetables is around the corner."

14. After spending years in a labor camp, a Soviet dissident was finally being allowed to emigrate to the U.S. Applying for work in a factory, he was told by the foreman, "It's a forty-hour week, eight hours a day, with weekends off."

"Thank you very much, sir," said the Russian, "but I was looking for a full-time job."

15. Q: What is the Leningrad String Quartet?
A: The Leningrad Symphony Orchestra after a tour of America.

16. Q: How can you tell whether it was scientists or politicians who introduced communism to Russia?

A: Scientists would have had the decency to try it on rats first.

17. Noticing a man walking down the street with only one shoe, a woman said, "Excuse me, but do you realize you've lost a shoe?"

    Smiling, the man said, "You are mistaken. I've found one."

18. An American, a Frenchman, and a Russian were discussing the meaning of the word "happiness."

    "For me," said the American, "happiness is putting my family in the car, driving into the country, and finding a quaint inn."

    The Frenchman said, "*Pour moi*, happiness is being with my girlfriend by the banks of a lake, picnicking late into the day on wine, cheese, and warm bread."

    The Russian said, "And for me, happiness is sitting in my room in Moscow. And when KGB comes knocking on the door, asking, 'Are you Sergei Cherganyev?', it is happiness for me to be able to say, '*Nyet*! He lives next door.'"

19. Q: Name four reasons crops fail in Russia.
    A: Winter, spring, summer, and fall.

20. Smarting from accusations that they'd been responsible for the assassination attempt on the life of Pope John Paul II in 1981, the

Soviets launched their own investigation into the matter.

After extensive interviews with would-be assassin Mahmet Agca, and countless viewings of the videotapes, they came to the conclusion that the pope opened fire first.

21. While on a trip to America, a Russian tourist was shown around an American home. After walking through it, the Soviet said, "My family's place is much the same—but without all these troublesome stairs and partitions."

22. "Tell me," one Afghan merchant asked another, "are the Soviet soldiers considered our friends or our brothers?"

"Our brothers, naturally," said the other. "One can *choose* one's friends."

23. The Polish head of the Communist party came to Moscow to meet with the secretary general. While he was there, he bought a magnificent full-length coat.

After landing back in Poland, he put on the coat and found that it barely reached to the middle of his thigh.

"Look at this," he said, "I've been cheated! When I was in Moscow, this was a full-length coat!"

"When you were in Moscow," his wife reminded him, "you were on your knees."

24. A factory worker in East Germany went to the bank to deposit his week's wages.

"Tell me," he said to the clerk, "would would happen to this deposit if the bank went out of business?"

"All deposits are guaranteed by the ministry of finance."

"And if that were overwhelmed with failing banks?"

"Then the government would make good on the ministry's obligations."

"And if the government were too greatly in debt?"

"Why, then, our brothers in the Soviet Union would help us in our time of need."

"And if the Soviet government collapsed?"

The teller looked around. "Fool!" he snarled. "Isn't that worth the loss of a week's wages?"

25. Then there was the stirring speech Gorbachev gave to the Politburo after assuming the reins of power. "Those who do not follow me," said he, "will follow comrades Brezhnev, Andropov, and Chernenko. . . ."

## SADISM

1. There have been many cruel people throughout history, but no one tops the man who was so mean he enjoyed reading Horatio Alger novels backward.

2. Q: What do you call a prostitute who works for a sadist?

A: Someone who's strapped for cash.

**SALESPEOPLE**  See also THE POLISH 4, RUSSIANS 13, SEX 31

1. Working in the pastry section of a grocery store, a young clerk was surprised when a huge man came up and asked for half a pie.

   "I'm sorry, sir, but I can't sell you just half a pie."

   Flushing with anger, the man told him to go and check with the department manager.

   Shaking his head, the clerk went to the cookie aisle, where he found the manager taking inventory. "Sir," he said, "there's this real asshole who wants to buy just half a pie." Just as he finished speaking, the clerk turned and noticed that the customer had followed him. Smiling, the clerk continued, "And this gentleman wishes to buy the other half."

2. Q: How can you tell when salespeople are lying?

A: Their lips move.

3. For as long as Chuck could remember, Clarence sold newspapers on Chicago's windy streets. On a particularly cold day Chuck shivered as he paid for the paper and said, "I d-don't know

how you do it, Clarence. After five minutes out here, I'd be c-crying from the cold."

"Ah, it's no problem," Clarence said. "Selling all these papers keeps up the circulation."

4. Then there was the coal salesperson who got into an argument with the home-heating-oil rep.

"How can you say your product is better?" the oil man asked.

"Simple," said the coal executive. "Ours is a product which not only goes to the buyer, but to the cellar."

## SANTA CLAUS

*See also* CHRISTMAS

1. Knock, knock
Who's there?
Centipede
Centipede who?
Centipede down the chimney

2. Tired of being called elves, the toymakers of the North Pole banded together and demanded a loftier, more professional sounding title. Santa obliged, telling them that henceforth he would refer to them as subordinate clauses. . . .

3. Then there was the relatively unknown Randolph the brown-nosed reindeer. Seems he was just as fleet as the rest of the team, but had trouble stopping. . . .

*See also* COLLEGE, GRAMMAR,
SEX EDUCATION, BLACKS 2, MORONS 6,
NUMBERS 2, POLISH 2, 3, RUSSIANS 11, 12

1. It was the first day of school, and the teacher was going around the classroom asking each of the children to spell their names.

   "D-O-R-I-S L-E-H-I-G-H," said one, and the teacher dutifully recorded it in her attendance book.

   "T-I-M M-O-R-I-A-R-T-Y," said another.

   "E-L-S-I-E," said another.

   "No," the teacher told the girl, "I need your whole name."

   "Oh," said the girl. "V-A-G-I-N-A."

2. "All right, Eustace," the teacher said to the fifth grader, "let's see you count."

   Holding out his hand, Eustace counted off the digits. "One, two, three, four, five."

   Smiling, the teacher said, "Very good, but can you count any higher?"

   Lifting his hand over his head, the boy started over again.

3. Standing in front of the class, the teacher begins the day's English lesson.

   "Adjectives," she says. "I want you all to select one, and then use it in a sentence."

   The first person she calls on is Edna, who says, "White. The walls are painted white."

"Very good," the teacher says, and calls on Wally.

"Big," he says. "Paul Bunyan was very big."

"Excellent," she smiles, and calls on RJ.

"Urinate," he says without hesitation.

"RJ!" she screams. "How could you?"

"What's wrong?" says the boy. "Urinate, but if you had your nose fixed, you'd be a ten."

4. When little Ned walked into the house, his mother asked him how his math test went.

"Fine," he said. "I nearly got a hundred."

"That's great! What did you get—a 98?"

"No. Two zeroes."

5. In order to get her sixth-grade class to study, the teacher came up with an innovative plan: she'd ask them a difficult question every Friday morning. If anyone could answer it, the entire class would get the rest of the day off.

The first Friday she asked, "Can anyone tell me the square root of 4?"

No one answered and, groaning, the students continued with their studies for the day.

The next Friday she asked, "Can anyone tell me how many planets in the solar system have rings?"

Once again, no one answered, and the students were forced to stay for the entire day.

Frustrated, on the following Friday one child brought a pair of black marbles to school. Just as the teacher was about to ask the question, the boy flipped them along the floor. Scowling, the teacher snapped, "All right! Who's the comedian with the two black balls."

"Eddie Murphy" the kid shouted. "See ya Monday!"

6. "Mary," said the teacher, "I'd like you to come up to the map and point out Cuba to me."

"Yes, sir," Mary said, and pointed to the island.

"Very good. Now, Alexander, tell us who discovered Cuba."

The boy replied, "Mary, sir."

7. For some reason, everyone but Lenore got the wrong answer on the science test.

"Tell me," the teacher asked her after returning the papers, "how did you know that heat causes objects to expand, and cold causes them to shrink?"

"Because I'm no dope," she said. "In the summer, when it's hot, the days are longer. And in the winter, when it's cold, they're shorter."

8. The second-grade teacher got up in front of the class and said, "Today, children, we're going to play a game. I'm going to hold something behind my back and describe it, and you have to guess what it is."

Reaching into a bag and holding an object

behind her, she said, "This is round and yellow."

"A tennis ball?" guessed little Vicki.

"No," said the teacher, "it's a grapefruit. But it shows you were thinking." She reached into the bag again and withdrew another object. "All right, class, this is long and yellow."

"A banana?" said young Gladys.

"No," said the teacher, "it's a pencil. But it shows you were thinking."

Suddenly, streetwise Tyrone raised his hand. "Say, do you mind if I try doin' one?"

The teacher said that that would be fine, and Tyrone turned his back to the class.

"Okay," he said, "what I got in my hand is about an inch long and has a red tip."

"Tyrone!" the teacher yelled.

"No, it's a match. But it shows you were thinkin'!"

9. "Now," said the teacher, "we all know that a one-L lama is a priest in Tibet. And a two-L llama is an animal found in South America. Can anyone tell me if there is such a thing as a three-L llama?"

Little Teri blurted, "Sure there is! It's a heckuva fire!"

10. Looking over at the least competent speller in the class, the English teacher said, "Here's an easy one, Rufus. Spell 'weather.' "

Pulling at his chin, Rufus said gamely, "W-E-T-H-O-R," and smiled.

Sighing, the teacher said, "Rufus, that's the worst spell of weather we've had here for quite some time."

11. Unfortunately, the popular English teacher came down with the flu and had to be hospitalized. There, she received countless get-well cards addressed to the ill literate. . . .

12. Then there was the College of Cosmetics, which allowed its students to take makeup exams. . . .

13. Taking her kindergarten class to the petting zoo, Mrs. Ganio gave each child a turn identifying the animals. Finally it was young Bess's turn. Pointing to a deer, the teacher asked, "Now what is the name of that animal?"

Bess looked long and hard, but was unable to come up with an answer.

"Think," the teacher encouraged. "What does your mommy call your daddy at home?"

Suddenly the girl's face brightened. "So *that's* what a horse's ass looks like!"

## SEALS

1. "Frankly," said Mr. Kent, "I feel perfectly fine. It's my wife who insisted I come and see you."

"What seems to be the problem?"

"It's my seals. I love them, and I honestly

don't see anything wrong with keeping them in the bathtub."

"I see. And, uh—what do you do with these seals when you bathe?"

Mr. Kent shot the doctor a surprised look. "Why, I blindfold them, naturally."

2. Q: What does Mr. Tupperware and a walrus have in common?
   A: Both thrive on a tight seal.

3. Q: What do they call it when a denizen of Sea World gets a hernia?
   A: Loose seal ball.

## SENIOR CITIZENS

See also MARRIAGE 2, PARTIES 1, PODIATRISTS 1, SEX 11, 14, SPERM BANKS 1

1. Mrs. Finlay had been going to the same corner grocery for years. Thus, when she suddenly started buying cat food, the grocer couldn't help but notice.

   "Have a new addition to the family, eh?" he asked.

   "No," the woman replied, "it's for my husband."

   "For Mark? My goodness, Mrs. Finlay, you shouldn't be feeding him cat food. It'll kill him."

   "I know, but it's all he'll eat."

Every week the woman would come in and buy more and more cat food. Suddenly, one week she didn't buy any. When the grocer asked why, she said in a quiet voice, "He . . . he's dead."

The grocer shook his head. "You see? I told you the cat food would kill him."

"Oh no," Mrs. Finlay said, "it wasn't the cat food. He broke his neck trying to lick his ass."

2. When elderly Waldo walked into the house of ill-repute, the madam looked him up and down.

"Say, old-timer, just what do you expect to do in here?"

"I intend, madam, to get laid."

"Oh yeah?" she tittered. "And how old are you."

He drew himself erect. "Ninety-five."

The madam said, "Ninety-five? Old-timer, you've *had* it."

He scratched his head. "Really? In that case, how much do I owe you?"

3. Q: What do women and dog poop have in common?

A: The older they get, the easier they are to pick up.

4. "You just can't win," one elderly man said to another as they walked through the park. "When I was a youngster, everyone told me to listen to the advice and ideas of old people."

He sighed. "Now that I'm old, everyone tells me I should listen to the advice and ideas of young people."

## SEPTIC TANKS    *See also* DEFECATION, LAVATORIES

1. Barry had been hired to clean the Kaplans' septic tank, and though no one was at home, he decided to do the job. Unfortunately, while lowering the hose into the open hole, he slipped and fell in. While floundering in the muck, he began shouting, "Fire! Fire!" as loud as he could.

   A neighbor heard him and phoned the fire department. When the firefighters arrived, they looked at Barry with disgust.

   "So where's the fire?" one man asked.

   "There isn't one," replied Barry. "But if I'd yelled, 'Shit! Shit!', who'd've come and saved me?"

**SEX**
See also BIRTH CONTROL, CONDOMS,
DATING, GENITALS, HONEYMOONS, IMPOTENCE,
INCEST, INFIDELITY, MARRIAGE, MASTURBATION,
MISTRESSES, NYMPHOMANIACS, ORGASMS,
PORNOGRAPHY, PROSTITUTES, SEX EDUCATION,
SEX TOYS, SODOMY, SPERM BANKS, SWINGING,
TOPLESS BARS, VENEREAL DISEASES, VIRGINITY,
VOYEURISM, ADAM AND EVE 5, AIRPLANES 1,
BASEBALL 1, 2, CASTAWAYS 1, CLERGY 3, 5,
CONFESSION 1, COURT-MARTIALS 1,
DEATH 1, 2, DRUGS 1, DRUNKS 4, EXECUTION 3,
EXTRATERRESTRIALS 4, 5, 6, FISHING 1, FOOTBALL 9,
GERMS 1, GOLF 4, GRANDPARENTS 1, HEAVEN 1,
HOSPITALITY 1, JEWISH AMERICAN PRINCESSES 2, 3, 13,
KIDS 3, LAWYERS 8, LIBRARIES 1, LIGHT BULBS 1, 3,
LITERATURE 4, MAIDS 2, MORONS 2, 4,
MOTION PICTURES 1, 2, 3, MURDER 3,
POLITICIANS 1, 7, 8, PRESIDENTS 1, PSYCHIATRISTS 5,
SQUIRRELS 1, WASPS 1, YUPPIES 1

1. The stoned young couple were necking on the sofa. Taking a hit during a break in the action, the woman said, "Hey, lover, what are you thinking about?"

   "The same thing you are," he replied.

   The woman grinned. "Great! I'll race you to the refrigerator!"

2. Arrius and Sextus bumped into each other in the street. "Hail, Sextus! I just met the happiest Roman I have ever seen. He was at the orgy last night."

"Gladiator?"

Arrius smiled. "You bet he is!"

3. Mary was a new girl at the orphanage. When her fifteen-year-old roommate Jo asked her how old she was, Mary replied, "I'm either ten, or fourteen—we're not sure."

"Let me ask you this," said Jo. "What's the best thing you ever put in your mouth?"

Mary smiled. "Oh, that would have to be chocolate ice cream in a sprinkle-cone."

Jo said, "You're ten."

4. Then there was the man who told a friend that sex with his wife was like the Fourth of July.

"You mean, fireworks and Roman candles?"

"No," he said. "I mean it happens just once a year."

5. "Say," said the newlywed to a friend at the office, "does your wife close her eyes when you're making love?"

"Sure does," the man said. "She just hates to see me having a good time."

6. It was their first date, and wanting to make a good impression on the lovely young woman, Edward walked her to the door and asked, "Is there anything else you'd like before I leave?"

"Yes," she said, "I want you to weigh me."

Surprised but nonetheless anxious to oblige, he drove her to the drugstore, pushed a penny into the scale, and allowed her to weigh herself. When he took her back home, the girl found her mother waiting up for her."

"Hello, dear," she said. "How was your date?"

The girl answered, "Wousy."

7. Frustrated because her boyfriend only wanted oral sex, Barbara was told by a friend to try rubbing garlic on her pussy. Barbara agreed to try, and the next day her friend asked her how it went.

"Terrible," she said. "He left and came back to bed with lettuce, tomatoes, and olive oil."

8. Q: What do light and hard have in common?
   A: You can't sleep with a light on, either.

9. Mrs. Brown said to her friend, "My Arthur will be in the hospital for several weeks."

"My dear," said the friend. "You've seen the doctor?"

"No," Mrs. Brown answered. "The nurse."

10. Every night at nine o'clock, George went to the corner bar for a drink. And every night, Harold, one of the ugliest men he had ever seen, was sitting at a table in the back, a different woman on his arm.

"How the hell does he do it?" George finally asked the bartender. "I mean, the guy's a real gargoyle!"

"Beats me too," the bartender said. "He just orders a beer, sits in the back, and once in a while grabs peanuts from the bar with his tongue."

11. Then there was the young woman who complained to a friend about the quality of sex with her ninety-year-old husband.

    "It's the same thing," she sighed, "weak in, weak out."

12. Then there was the farmer's daughter who got a bad reputation because she couldn't keep her calves together.

13. Not that he was single-minded, but the antique dealer would only make love to women when they were menstruating. As he explained it to a friend, he liked nothing more than a period piece.

14. Young Raleigh cornered his widower grandfather at the old man's wedding.

    "Grampa, I know you're lonely, but how can you do this?"

    "Do what?"

    "Marry Bambi! She's a lovely person, but— you're eighty-two and she's only nineteen. Don't you realize that making love to a woman like that could be fatal?"

    The old man shrugged. "I'm a fatalist, Raleigh, and if she dies—she dies!"

15. "I found it," chortled George as he stopped by the office of his coworker Perry. "The fool-proof way to extraordinary lovemaking!"

"I could sure use a few pointers," Perry admitted. "Lately my wife hasn't been satisfied. And sex has really been tiring me out."

"Then here's what you do. You make love to her, roll over, and get a good fifteen minutes' sleep. Then when you wake up, make love to her again. You'll be a new man. I made love to my wife four times last night!"

Perry was impressed and agreed to try it. That night he and his wife got into bed, and Perry grabbed her. He made wild love, napped, got up, and grabbed her again. She was stunned but thrilled. Afterward, he napped again, then got up, ravaged her once more, and went to sleep again. When he awoke, he glanced at the clock.

"Dammit!" he yelled, "I'm ten minutes late for work!" Pulling on his clothes, he raced to the office. When he arrived, his boss called him into her office.

"Sorry, Mrs. Gable," Perry said, "but in ten years, I've never once been late for work. Please forgive me for these ten minutes."

"Ten minutes?" Mrs. Gable exclaimed. "Where the hell were you Wednesday and Thursday?"

16. Q: What's the difference between a nice girl and a good girl?
   A: A nice girl goes home and goes to bed. . . .

17. Marge fixed her friend Janice up with a blind date. After a pleasant dinner the couple made love. Afterward, obviously disappointed, the woman frowned at her companion.

"Just where are you *from*, anyway?" she asked.

"I am Hungarian," he replied.

"Shit. I thought Marge meant you were from Gary."

18. "I can't *stand* it," one priest said to another. "Thoughts about sex preoccupy me day and night!"

Trying to be helpful, his companion said, "Maybe you ought to take a cold shower!"

"No good," the first priest wailed, "I've taken so many cold showers, whenever it rains I get an erection!"

19. While walking home from the factory, Goddard saw a woman weeping uncontrollably.

"What's wrong?" he asked, putting an arm around her shoulder.

"It's horrible," she sobbed, "just horrible. Jerome is dead!"

Feeling that there was little he could do, Goddard walked on. A few minutes later, he came across another woman crying hysterically.

"Jerome is dead!" she screamed as she staggered past.

Continuing along the road, Goddard came to a sickening sight: a big bear of a man lay on the road beneath the wheels of a truck. The force of the impact had ripped his clothes off and, much to Goddard's surprise, the man had a penis over a foot long. There were several other women standing around him, all of them sobbing from the heart, "Jerome is dead! Jerome is dead!"

Upon reaching his house, he said to his wife, "Honey, you won't believe what I just saw. A man was lying in the road, stiff as a board—and he had an endowment at least fourteen inches long.

"Sweet Jesus," his wife exclaimed, "Jerome is dead?"

20. "Why are you taking so long?" the woman asked her husband.

"I'm sorry," he replied, "but I just can't think of anyone!"

21. Not long after sexy young divorcee Stella moved in across the street, Parker began spending more and more time there—helping, he told his wife, with difficult chores. It didn't take long for his wife to become suspicious, however, and one day after he'd been gone for several hours, she picked up the phone and called.

"Stella," she yelled, "you tell my husband to get his ass across the street!"

"What a coincidence," Stella said. "That's exactly what he's been doing for weeks now!"

22. Because it took nearly an hour and six cups of coffee to get him going in the morning, Mr. Elliot went to see his doctor.

"As near as I can determine," said the doctor, "your problem is fatigue. Since you don't exercise, I suggest you cut back on your sex life."

"Fine," said Mr. Elliot. "Which half should I stop—talking about it, or thinking about it?"

23. Then there were the golden shower fetishists who were fond of chanting, "We're number one! We're number one!"

24. As Jack and Jill were walking up a hill, Jill cast sidelong glances at Jack, who was holding a pitchfork, a bucket, a chicken, and a rope which was attached to a goat.

After a few minutes Jill said, "I don't mind telling you, Jack, that walking alone with you like this makes me nervous."

"Why?" asked the young man.

"Oh—you might just try to have your way with me," she said.

Jack scowled. "That's crazy! I've got my hands full."

"I know," said Jill, "but you could stick the pitchfork in the ground, tie the goat to it, lay the chicken down, and put the bucket on top of it, couldn't you?"

25. After having suffered a heart attack, Mr. Richter was told to cut back on his sexual activity.

"A good rule of thumb," his doctor said, "is to only have sex on days of the week with an *r* in them."

Thanking him, Mr. Richter went home and explained the situation to his wife.

Thursday, Friday, and Saturday passed with the couple's typically passionate bouts of love-making. After skipping a day, however, Mrs. Richter began to feel itchy. Lying in bed for several hours, she finally turned and woke her husband.

"I need you," she whispered into his ear as her hand found its way into his pants.

Still half-asleep, Mr. Richter asked, "Wh-what day is it?"

She replied, "Mondray."

26. Taking the woman back to his hotel room, the conventioneer went to put twenty-five cents in a slot above the bed.

"What are you doing?" the woman asked.

"Well," said the man, "when you put a quarter in, the bed will start to vibrate."

The woman cooed, "Forget it, love. When you get a quarter in, I'll do plenty of vibrating."

27. Going to the drugstore, the woman asked the pharmacist what would help get rid of her husband's dandruff. He recommended *Head and Shoulders*.

The next day she returned and he asked how the treatment was going.

"Fine, I guess," she said, "only how do you give 'shoulder'?"

28. Marrying shortly before Easter, the couple crawled into bed and the man began to fondle his wife. Much to his surprise and consternation, she didn't respond.

"I'm sorry," she says, "but I can't make love to you now."

"Why?" he demanded.

"Because it's Lent."

Furious, the husband screamed, "Oh yeah? To who and for how long?"

29. Of course, you know you've been married a bit too long if your wife gives up sex for Lent and you don't find out until well after Easter.

30. Retiring to the apartment of the famed football player, the young woman was crushed when she saw him sit down, take off his clothes, and scratch his toes.

"Shit!" she moaned. "I thought you said you had *at least* a foot!"

31. After a long, hard day on the road, a traveling salesman stopped at a farm and knocked on the door.

"Excuse me, sir," he said to the farmer, "but is there any possibility that I might stay the night?"

The farmer scratched his head. "Y'can," he

said, "but it'll be a little cramped. Ya'll have to sleep with my son Luke."

The salesman frowned. "Just my luck. I come all this way and I'm in the wrong damned joke."

## SEX EDUCATION                    See also SEX

1. It was fine with parents when the school board announced that they were beginning a program of sex education. However, more than one parent protested when they learned that the tests would all be oral.

## SEX TOYS                         See also SEX

1. After browsing through the sex shop, Mr. Baker decided to purchase an artificial vagina.

   "Excuse me, sir," the clerk asked, "but exactly how do you intend to use this?"

   Recoiling, Mr. Baker declared, "That, son, is none of your affair!"

   Shrugging, the clerk said, "Suit yourself, but I was only trying to save you some money."

   "How?" Mr. Baker demanded.

   "Well, sir," he replied, "I don't have to charge sales tax on food items."

2. Then there's the canny businessperson who is opening a store which sells only vibrators. The name? Toys for Twats.

1. When the rod in the closet fell from the weight of all her clothes, Mrs. Ramer decided to give some of her wardrobe to the Salvation Army. While she was gathering together garments she no longer wore, she searched the pockets; in one coat she found a ticket for shoes she'd brought in for repair nearly six years before.

   "So *that's* what happened to those," she muttered. Later that day, while dropping off the clothes, she decided to see if the repairman still had the shoes.

   After studying the ticket, the man said, "I'm sorry, but those won't be ready until Friday."

2. Walking down the street, the moron noticed a sign in a shoe repair shop: BOOTS POLISHED INSIDE. Going in, he walked up to the clerk.

   "I don't need my boots polished," he said, "but I've got a question. How do you keep the polish from getting on peoples' socks?"

3. The man asked quietly, "Is it in?"

   "Yes," the woman replied.

   "Does it hurt?"

   "N-no," she said. "It feels *wonderful!*"

   Smiling, the clerk said, "Shall I throw out your old shoes, then?"

1. Hearing a scream from the playroom, the mother rushed in and found her infant daughter pulling the hair of her four-year-old brother.

   After separating them, the mother said to her son, "Don't be upset with your sister, honey. She didn't know she was hurting you."

   No sooner had the mother returned to her chores than she heard more screaming. This time she rushed in and found the baby crying.

   "Now what happened?" she said.

   "Nothing," said the boy, "except that now she knows."

2. Then there was the mother whose kids were so hostile toward one another that she didn't refer to it as sibling rivalry, but sible war.

**SKUNKS**                         *See also* ANIMALS 1

1. He was a nearsighted skunk, and he spent nearly an hour holding a conversation with a fart.

2. Not only was the skunk nearsighted, but he was parsimonious as hell: he absolutely refused to part with a scent.

1. It was his first time at skydiving class, and Joey was thrilled.

   "What you have to do," the instructor said, "is jump, count to ten, then pull the ripcord.

   So excited that he wasn't really paying attention, Joey said, "P-p-p-p-pardon m-m-m-m-me, wh-wh-wh-wh-what w-w-w-was th-th-th-that n-n-n-n-number ag-ag-agin?"

   "Two" the instructor replied.

2. Burton finally got to jump, and after leaping from the plane, he pulled his ripcord. Much to his horror, the chute failed to deploy.

   Refusing to panic, Burton pulled his emergency cord. Again nothing happened.

   Now he panicked. Just then, however, he saw a woman rushing up toward him. Hope filled his breast, and when she was within shouting distance, Burton hollered, "Hey! Do you know anything about parachutes?"

   "No!" the woman shouted back. "Do you know anything about gas ovens?"

3. During the height of hostilities during World War II, a Polish freedom fighter volunteered to go behind enemy lines and spy on the Germans. Late one night, in England, he crawled into the belly of a B-17 for the flight over German-occupied Poland.

When he reached his destination, he pulled on a parachute and jumped. Unfortunately, when he pulled the ripcord, nothing happened.

"Why don't these operations ever go as planned?" he complained as he fell. "Shit. And I'll bet there won't even be anyone to meet me when I arrive."

## SNORING

1. "Dr. Stenson," the woman said, "you have to do something for my husband. As soon as he falls asleep, he starts to snore like some kind of monster."

   "He may need an operation. Does it really bother you that much?"

   "Me?" she said. "It bothers the entire congregation!"

## SODOMY      *See also* ARABS 1, PIGS 2, ROYALTY 1

1. While driving through Kansas, a ventriloquist got a flat tire. Stopping at a farm to use the phone, he decided to have some fun with the yokels. After calling AAA, he made one of the cows talk to the farmer's wife. Then he had one of the pigs complain to the farmer about the accommodations.

   All the while, the farmer's son was uneasy. Finally, after the horse asked for more hay, the boy blurted, "If the sheep says anything about me, it's a goddamn lie!"

2. Hoping to emulate her idol, Margaret Mead, anthropology graduate student Sherry Berne went deep into the Appalachian Mountains to interview people who were utterly cut off from civilization. Three days into the hills, she found a handsome young man living in a small log cabin. In exchange for a pack of gum, he agreed to answer her questions.

"First," she said, "I haven't seen a woman within miles of this place. What do you do for sexual gratification?"

"Well," he said around a thick wad of gum, "there's my horse Hortense over there—"

"You mean you actually make love to your horse?"

"Yes'm. And did you see the creek when ya'll came on up? Well, I kin usually find a duck down there—"

"Dear!"

"No," he said mournfully, "they're dolls, but they run too fuckin' fast."

3. Q: What did they call the scandal with the congressional pages?
   A: Tailgate.

4. Three men were walking back from the fishing hole. Spotting a sheep in the meadow, one man said, "Damn. If only it was Bo Derek."

The other said, "If only it was Morgan Fairchild."

The third said, "If only it was dark."

5. Then there was the San Francisco lawyer who got his client's sodomy charge reduced to "following too closely."

## SPEECH IMPEDIMENTS

See also THE HANDICAPPED, SEX 6, SKYDIVING 1

1. Putting his stethoscope to the young woman's chest, the doctor said, "Big breaths, dear."

She smiled. "Yup. And I'm not even thixteen yet!"

## SPERM BANKS

1. The vain old octogenarian insisted on making a deposit in the sperm bank. Though the nurse tried to dissuade him, suggesting that he may not be up to the task, he was adamant.

Two hours later, he still hadn't emerged from the men's room, and the nurse went to the door.

"Sir, are you all right?"

Panting heavily, the man wheezed, "I—I tried to do it with my left hand, then with my right. Nothing! Christ, I even tried smacking it against the sink several times!"

Panicking, the nurse ran to get a doctor, who ordered the old man to admit him.

"Sorry to cause so much trouble," the old man said, opening the door, "but I'll be damned if I can get the cap off this friggin' bottle!"

2. Then there's the sperm bank which intends to impregnate women using aerosol jets. The name of the process? Heir spray.

3. Q: What is the slang phrase being used to describe artificial insemination?
   A: A technical knock-up.

4. Wanting to leave something of himself for posterity, the achingly handsome movie star went to a sperm bank to leave a deposit. The doctor sent him to a private room, though, not surprisingly, there was no shortage of nurses offering to assist him with his chore.

   When he finally returned with his specimen an hour later, the doctor asked what took him so long.

   "Sorry," he said, "but I spent most of the time getting Nurse Buttel to cough it back up."

5. Then there was the young woman who was fired from her job at the sperm bank after she became pregnant. Seems she was embezzling. . . .

6. Q: When representatives of sperm banks come to your door and ask for a donation, what is the proper way to refuse?
   A: "No, thanks. I give the united way."

7. Q: Why did the woman go to a sperm bank?
   A: She wanted an ice pop.

8. Then there's the lighthearted doctor who tries to put his patients at ease by using a patented, lifelike phallus for artificial insemination. The name? "The Phoney Baloney."

## SQUIRRELS

1. Q: What's the difference between squirrels and men?
   A: Squirrels put their nuts on a rock and crack them.

## STALIN          See also CASTRO, MUSSOLINI, RUSSIA

1. When Stalin fell out of official favor in 1956, his body was removed from Red Square. However, officials were at a loss as to what to do with it. Approaching the British ambassador, the Russians asked if Churchill's wartime ally could be interred in England.

   "Afraid not," the ambassador said. "Karl Marx is buried in England, you know, and having two such eminent communists would be excessive."

Turing to the East Germans, the Russians were refused by their ambassador as well. "We're still trying to live down Hitler. One dictator is quite enough."

The response from the Italians was the same. Learning of the Soviet plight, and wishing to score some points with the Russian rulers, the Israeli ambassador offered to allow Stalin to be buried in his nation.

"*Nyet!*" the Russians replied. "You people had a Resurrection once. . . ."

2. Then there were the American and Russian historians who were discussing ambitious leaders of the first half of the twentiety century.

"My vote goes to Herbert Hoover," said the American, "who tried to teach Americans to stop drinking."

"That's nothing," said the Russian. "I pick Josef Stalin, who tried to teach Russians to stop eating."

**THE STOCK MARKET**     *See also* THE DEFICIT,
DOCTORS 9

1. In the past, stocks split. Today they fall completely apart.

1. Then there was the moron who kept his sundial under a spotlight so he could tell time at night.

**SURGERY**     *See also* DOCTORS, PROSTITUTES 10, RACQUETBALL 1

1. Poor Mr. Melnick couldn't seem to get rid of the pains in his abdomen. He went in and had his appendix removed; then had a section of his ulcerous stomach removed; then had a spot of cancer scraped from his liver. And still he wasn't well.

   Finally Mrs. Melnick refused to allow him to undergo any more surgery. As she put it, "I'm tired of other people opening my male."

2. Waking after surgery, attorney Belzig was surprised to find all the shades drawn in the recovery room. Summoning a nurse, he asked him why.

   "Well, sir," the nurse said, "there's a fire raging in the building across the way, and your doctor didn't want you to think the operation had failed."

3. While reading on the beach with his wife, the abdominal surgeon suddenly reached over,

grabbed the book she was reading, and tore out the few pages of material following the last chapter.

"Sorry," he exclaimed. "Force of habit."

## SWINGING

*See also* SEX, GOLF 3

1. Inspired by the success of K-Mart, where lesser quality goods are sold, the owners of Plato's Retreat opened a club for swingers who are dogs. The name? Pluto's Retreat.

## TAMPONS

*See also* CONDOMS 3

1. Walking into a drugstore, two inner-city children asked the pharmacist for tampons.

The woman smiled. "Are these for your mother?"

"No," said one of the kids. "For us."

"For you? Whatever for?"

"It said on television that if you used them, you could swim and skate and do other nifty things."

2. Then there was the Greek military strategist who suggested using tampons to defend the nation. It would keep the Reds back, hold the Poles at bay, starve the French, and leave everyone at home happy.

1. So in love was she with Patrick Swayze and Tom Cruise that the woman had the actors' likenesses tatooed on her behind, one on each cheek.

   Her husband didn't mind, though when he went to pick her up at the tatoo parlor, he took one look and snorted, "They're terrible likenesses. They don't look anything like the actors."

   Looking for an impartial judgment, the woman stepped into the street and collared a bum. Bending over and exposing her cheeks, she said, "Tell me, whose faces are these?"

   The bum scratched his head. "Don't know about the dudes on either side," he said, "but the one in the middle is Willie Nelson."

*TEA*                              *See also* COFFEE

1. When a fast-food place opened across from her family restaurant, old Mrs. Toddy started losing business. Realizing that she had to cut corners, she decided to save money by using the same tea bags more than once to make tea.

   As it happened, a small group of Britons soon stopped coming in everyday at teatime. When Mrs. Toddy saw them going to the fast-food place, she ran over.

"What's wrong?" she asked. "Why don't you come to my place anymore?"

One of the Britons wagged a scolding finger. "Tut, tut, Mrs. Toddy. You should've known that honest tea is the best policy."

2. The intern rushed over to Room B, where the moronic Mr. Blowitz lay writhing in agony, his scrotum badly burned.

"Jesus," said the intern, "what did you do to yourself?"

"My doctor told me to give up coffee."

"So?"

"So I was making myself some tea," Blowitz moaned, "and all I did was follow the instructions."

"Which were—?"

" 'Before drinking, soak bag in boiling water.' "

## TEENAGERS                    See also KIDS

1. A teenager is someone who gets ten hours of sleep a day, none of it at night.

2. However, teenage girls and boys *are* different in one important respect: a girl puts lipstick on, while a boy wipes it off.

3. And, naturally, they're people who want to learn how to drive. When this happens, its the wise parent who doesn't stand in their way.

### TERRORISTS

1. It's rare, but it happened: a group of Jewish terrorists hijacked a plane. They ransomed it for five million dollars in pledges.

2. Then there were the Polish terrorists, who staged a raid on the Special Olympics.

### THANKSGIVING
*See also* CONFESSION 3, MASTURBATION 2

1. Distressed with how disobedient the young turkey was, the mother turkey declared, "If your father could see you now, he'd roll over in his gravy."

2. Not that the Puritans were thinking ahead, but if they'd shot a wildcat instead of a turkey, we'd all be eating pussy for dinner.

### TOBACCO
*See also* PSYCHIATRISTS 10

1. When Gina's date came to the door, the girl's mother was perturbed to see that the young man chewed tobacco. While her daughter finished getting dressed, her mother listened at the top of the steps. After a minute she shouted nervously downstairs.

"Excuse me, young man, but are you by any chance spitting into our Ming vase?"

"No ma'am," the youth replied, "but I'm gettin' closer each time."

2. As the sage pointed out, smokers are people who puff on cigarettes, cigars, and steps. . . .

## TOPLESS BARS
*See also* SEX

1. Q: What is the difference between a forgiving soul and a topless dancer?
   A: One has no axe to grind, the other no grinds to axe.

2. It was a sad, sad case: due to tough new laws, the topless bar was closed and the stripper was fired. She hasn't been obscene since.

3. Protesting violently, Nathan was tossed into a cell in the local jail. Grasping the bars, he continued to yell out deprecations as the police walked away.

   "Hey, calm down, man," said another man in the cell. "That ain't gonna get you out."

   "Out!" Nathan screamed. "I shouldn't be in here in the first place! My only crime was getting a hard-on anytime I saw a beautiful woman."

   "You didn't rape anyone? They locked you up just for getting a boner?"

"Well," Nathan said, "not exactly. You see, I was always seeing pretty girls at work or in the street, so to keep from being embarrassed, I began wearing a metal jockstrap. I forgot all about it, and went with a couple of friends to a topless bar."

"So?"

"So," Nathan said, "two dancers and the bartender were killed by shrapnel."

**TOURISTS**　　　　　*See also* COURTROOMS 1, 2, 3, LANGUAGES 6, LEPERS 8, RUSSIANS 5, 9, 21

1. "And how will I know," asked the traveler, "when I am leaving Scandinavia?"

   "Simple," said the villager. "When you come to the last Lapp, you'll be near the Finnish line."

2. After telling the customs agent he had nothing in his bags but clothing, Arnie was alarmed when the official decided to open them up and check. In the very first one she opened, cushioned between his socks was a bottle of cognac.

   "Nothing to declare but clothing, huh?"

   "Right," Arnie extemporized. "That, madam, is my nightcap."

3. Arriving in France, the busy American executive walked up to the registration desk in the

hotel. Making conversation, the clerk asked, "And how did you come over, madam?"

Shrugging, the woman replied, "I don't know. My secretary made all the arrangements."

4. Going into the travel agent's office, the moron said, "I'd like a round-trip ticket, please."

"Where to?" the agent asked.

"Why, back here, naturally."

5. While showing the busload of tourists the sights in Nevada, the guide says, "Ladies and gentlemen, we are now passing the only legal house of ill-repute in the country."

With a pained look on his face, a man in the back of the bus shouts, "Why?"

6. Walking up to a New Yorker, the gentleman from India said, "Pardon me. Which way to the Statue of Liberty, or should I go fuck myself?"

**TRAINS**     *See also* TOURISTS, COURTROOMS 8, HUNTERS 1, RUSSIANS 3

1. While touring New York, a Texan stopped at Grand Central Station.

"Y'know," he said to a conductor, "in Texas, you kin ride one of these for twenty-four hours straight and *still* be in Texas."

"Big deal," said the conductor. "We've got trains that run like that too."

2. "Conductor," said the passenger, "I have to get to New York. Should I take this train?"

"If you'd like," the conductor said, "but if you wait just a minute, the engineer will be along."

## TRUCKERS    See also ETIQUETTE 1, THE POLISH 8, 9

1. While driving down the highway, a trucker saw a pair of men hitchhiking. Only after he picked them up did he begin to suspect that they were gay.

After a few miles, one of the hitchhikers said, "I know this is terribly rude, but would you object if I farted?"

"Naw," the driver said, with overwrought macho, "go ahead."

Much to his surprise, the rider released a fart so powerful that the windows rattled and the radio knob skipped to the next station. His companion also farted then, a blast so mighty that the reclining seat actually slipped back a notch.

Amazed, but not to be outdone, the truck driver forced out a fart of his own, but was only able to muster a mousy-sounding squeak which drew giggles from the two hitchhikers.

"Well," said one, "we know who in this cab is a virgin!"

1. It was a black day for the dry-cleaners' union when a big corporation unveiled a home dry-cleaning product. In fact, the union leader was so upset he held a press conference. . . .

2. After picketing the bakery for just an hour, the bagel makers were given what they wanted: more dough. And it was just as well, since most of them were against the kneadless strike. . . .

3. Meanwhile, when it came to unionizing the laundry workers, the turnout was so great that people had to sit on bleachers.

4. Then there were the overworked custodians, who unionized, went to the local school district, and demanded sweeping reforms.

**VENEREAL DISEASES**     *See also* SEX, NYMPHOMANIACS 1

1. In a panic Chester phoned his physician. "I've got to see you quickly," he said. "I think I have the clap!"

   "All right," the doctor said, "make a date with my receptionist."

   "I did," Chester said, "which is the reason I gotta see you!"

2. Upon leaving his office, Dr. Koenig found Mr. Bojarski sobbing in the parking lot.

   "What's wrong?" the doctor asked.

   "What's wrong? Doctor, you should know! You're the one who told me my girlfriend has VD!"

   Dr. Koenig scratched his head, then grinned. "No, Mr. Bojarski. What I said was that the test results showed her pee's all right.' "

3. Suffering from the clap, the popular whore who worked the military base reluctantly told prospective clients about her infection. Undaunted, a not-very-bright colonel bought her for the entire evening, confident that he was immune to any disease of the privates.

4. Conducting interviews with new arrivals, St. Peter interviewed a black woman.

   "Name?" he asked.

   "Ellie."

   "Cause of death?"

   "Herpes."

   St. Peter looked up. "Madam, one does not die from herpes."

   Ellie replied, "You do when you give it to your husband Tank."

5. Then there's the growing group of herpes sufferers, known collectively as the American Lesion.

1. Because his trip to North America took so long, Leif Ericson returned home only to learn that his name had been crossed from the list of village inhabitants.

   He complained to the village chief, who relayed the adventurer's displeasure to his statistician.

   "I'm so sorry," said the latter. "I must have taken Leif off my census."

*VIRGINITY*          *See also* SEX, FOOTBALL 5,
                                HONEYMOONS 2, INCEST 1

1. Q: Why is virginity like a no-hitter?
   A: A hot stick can end them both.

2. Q: What's the difference between hemophilia and virginity?
   A: None. One prick, and it's all over.

*VOYEURS*          *See also* SEX

1. "I hear they got old Bronston looking into the girls' dorm," said one voyeur to another. "What a terrible thing to have happen."

   "Yes," said the other, "and right at the peek of his career!"

2. Extremely horny and extremely broke, Carlton went to the local brothel and begged the madam to extend him credit. She refused, though she did offer him a bargain: her pet chicken was in heat, and she'd allow Carlton to satisfy her for nothing.

Reluctantly Carlton allowed her to lead him to a room in the back. There, he found a bed, a mirror, and the chicken. After the door was shut, he said a few soft words to the fowl, then proceeded to screw it. Much to his surprise, he enjoyed the warm, tight bird, and hammered at it with wild abandon.

The next night, horny all over, he returned to the brothel. The madam said that the chicken had died, but because he *was* a good customer, she'd let him watch a sex show. Figuring that's better than nothing, Carlton went to a room where a group of men were huddled around a one-way mirror, laughing hysterically. Peeking over one man's shoulder, Carlton was aghast: inside a room he saw a man quietly having sex with a goose.

"Hey," he shouted, "I don't see what's so funny!"

"It's okay," one man said, "but it's nothing compared to the guy who went to town last night with the chicken."

## WALLPAPER

1. Delighted to learn that his new wallpaper was washable, the moron was furious when the very first time he washed it, it was snatched from the clothesline.

## WASPS

1. Sad but true: the WASP would only make love to her husband doggie-style. He would sit up and beg, then she would roll over and play dead.

## WEALTH
*See also* MISERS, WILLS,
DATING 3, ENGAGEMENTS 1, MARRIAGE 2

1. The oil magnates were walking through a Rolls Royce showroom, digesting their lunch, when one of them bent to look at a sticker on the side of a Corniche.

   "Seventy grand," he said. "Hell, it's a handsome car. I'm gonna buy it!"

   As he reached for his wallet, his companion put a hand on his arm.

   "No," he said, "let me get this one. You paid for lunch."

## THE WEATHER *See also* EXECUTION 5, SEX 18

1. "Yes," said the TV weather person, "we've had cold days up here in Minneapolis, but today was the worst. It's so cold, in fact, that the exhibitionists are describing themselves . . . ."

## WEST POINT *See also* THE MILITARY

1. Returning to West Point late one night, Colonel Smith and his wife were challenged by the sentry at the gate.

   "Halt and identify yourself!"

   "Jesus, Mary, and Joseph!" declared the startled woman.

   The sentry stepped aside. "Advance, Holy Family, to be recognized."

2. Then there was the gay cadet who was booted out of West Point. Seems he tried to switch majors. . . .

## WHALES

1. Q: What does it take to circumcize a whale?
   A: Fore skin divers.

1. When hyperactivity caused wealthy Mike Hunt to fade to a shadow of his former self, Dr. Kellog came to the rescue with a complex program of medication.

   Soon Hunt began to gain weight. His color returned, along with his old vigor. To make sure he didn't regress, Kellog put him on a regimen of pills and vitamins.

   "I just want you to know," said the grateful Hunt, "that for saving my life, I've put you in my will."

   Flattered, Dr. Kellog said, "Thanks. Now, before you go, there's a small change I'd like to make in the prescription I gave you."

2. Lying on his deathbed, the wealthy Mr. Beamish was instructing his attorney on last-minute changes in his will.

   "I wish to leave everything I own, all stocks, bonds, property, art, and money, to my wife. However, there is one stipulation."

   "And that is?"

   "In order to inherit, she must marry within six months of my death."

   The lawyer seemed puzzled. "Why make such an unusual request?"

   Mr. Beamish answered, "Because I want *someone* to be sorry I died."

3. When he was finished with the bulk of the changes, Mr. Beamish added yet one more stipulation to his will: that he be buried at sea.

   He explained, "That's just in case my wife makes good on her threat to dance on my grave."

4. Examining his new will, the old man said to his attorney, "I guess this makes my son and I sort of like football players."

   "How's that?" the lawyer asked.

   "Well, until I kick off, he doesn't receive."

5. Due to inherit a fortune when his sickly, widower father died, Winston decided he needed a woman to enjoy it with. Going to a singles' bar, he spotted a woman whose beauty took his breath away.

   "I'm just an ordinary accountant," he said, walking up to her, "but in just a week or two, my father will die and I'll inherit ten million dollars."

   The woman went home with Winston, and the next day she became his stepmother.

6. Then there was the rich old man who decided to spend every penny on himself, thus turning his heirs gray. . . .

*See also* ADAM AND EVE 4,
BIGAMY 1, CHILDBIRTH 2, COWS 1, FOOD 2, 3,
GHOSTS 2, LADY GODIVA 1, LAVATORIES 5,
LITERATURE 1, PANHANDLERS 1, PARTIES 3,
PHILOSOPHERS 1, PROGRESS 3, 4, 5, PROSTITUTES 8,
SANTA CLAUS 1, SURGERY 1, TEA 1,
TOURISTS 1, VIKINGS 1

1. Though their parents had a prosperous cattle ranch, the two brothers decided to leave home and start a spread of their own. After buying land and acquiring steer, they phoned home with just one request: they wanted to know what to name it.

   "Simple," said their mother. "Call it 'Focus.' "

   "Focus?" squawked one of the boys. "Whatever for?"

   "Because," she responded, "that's where the sun's rays meet."

2. Then there was the glassblower who inhaled and got a pane in the stomach.

3. Q: What's the difference between a marine and a pair of broken cars?
   A: One goes to sea, the others cease to go.

4. Q: What's the difference between a Xerox machine and the flu?
   A: One makes facsimiles, the other makes sick families.

5. Q: What's the difference between a summer jacket worn in the winter, and a pulled molar?

   A: One is too thin, the other is tooth out.

6. Q: What's the difference between an apartment dweller and someone with just a father or mother?

   A: One has to pay rents, and the other doesn't.

7. The Greek scholar took his torn pants to the Greek tailor. Studying the tear, the tailor asked, "Euripedes?"

   The scholar nodded. "Eumenides?"

8. Knock, knock.
   Who's there?
   Eskimo, Christian, Italian.
   Eskimo, Christian, Italian who?
   Eskimo, Christian, Italian no lies.

9. Q: What's the difference between a woman in a church and a woman in a bathtub?

   A: One has hope in her soul. . .

10. The mole family was burrowing through the ground when all of a sudden, papa mole ran smack into a rock. As a result, mama mole stopped short, as did baby mole, leaving them both deep in molasses. . . .

11. Passing the nurse as he arrived at the hospital, the doctor cauterize and smiled. She, intern, smiled back.

12. When a warming trend hit the Arctic, scientists were assigned to watch glaciers in danger of splitting. Naturally, all of the researchers had to have good ice sight.

13. Then there was the sage who realized that winter seems like the longest season because it comes in one year and out the other.

14. Feeling dizzy, the elderly man walked into the drug store. Spotting a white-jacketed young man behind a counter, he walked over. Unknown to the old gentleman, the youth was the soda jerk, not the pharmacist.

    "I don't feel well," said the old man. "Are you a doctor?"

    "In a way," said the boy, proudly. "I'm a fizzician."

15. Returning home from a hard day in the Tibetan fields, San Wu found his wife asleep on the mat. He kissed her, and was surprised when she suddenly sniffed, rose, and bolted for the kitchen.

    "What's wrong?" San asked.

    His wife cried, "Oh, my baking yak!"

16. Falling in love with a woman who rode the train every day, the ticket salesman asked her to marry him. She accepted, and, quite naturally, they had their reception on the train platform above the station. Unfortunately, the combined weight of the guests caused the platform to collapse.

The moral: Never marry above your station.

17. Moving to Shanghai, the Americans missed many things—but above all, they yearned for a fireplace. Though the Chinese didn't have fireplaces, they agreed to put one in for the Americans, and did a lousy job of it. The first time the Americans lit it, the smoke didn't go up the chimney, but came pouring out the front of the fireplace and into the house. Coughing, their eyes tearing, the Americans finally managed to open the windows.

The next day the father couldn't go to work, and the children didn't go to school. As the American explained it to his boss over the phone, "I'm sorry, sir, but we're all incapacitated due to the Asian flue."

18. Q: What's the difference between a Boy Scout and a man who fixes bicycle horns?
A: The Boy Scout's motto is "Be Prepared." The other's motto is "Beep Repaired."

1. At the beginning of the war the superstitious Hitler asked his astrologer to predict the outcome of the war.

   "We don't need a chart for that," the astrologer said, "just a coin."

   "A coin?" said Hitler.

   "Yes. You must flip it. If it lands on heads, then the Fatherland will win. If it lands on tails, then the English will win."

   "And if," Hitler says, "it lands on its edge?"

   "In that case," the astrologer replied, "it's a miracle, and Poland will win."

2. It's a little-known fact, but there was actually a kamikaze pilot who survived the fierce Battle of Midway. His name: Chicken Teriyaki.

3. Shortly before the blitzkrieg, the Polish soldiers were being briefed by their captain.

   "As you know, men, ammunition is short. Thus, answer this question: if you were confronted by a German soldier and a Russian soldier, which one would you shoot?"

   Private Ostrovsky answered, "The German, sir."

   "Why?"

   The soldier replied, "Business before pleasure, sir."

1. He meant no harm, but after the doctor X-rayed his patient's cervix, she had the distinct feeling that she'd been ultraviolated. . . .

## YUPPIES

1. Q: Why do Yuppies feel that sex is counter-productive?
   A: Because you start at the top and work your way to the bottom.

# PENGUIN PUTNAM

online

Your Internet gateway to a virtual environ-
ment with hundreds of entertaining and
enlightening books from Penguin Putnam Inc.

*While you're there, get the latest buzz on
the best authors and books around—*

Tom Clancy, Patricia Cornwell, W.E.B. Grif-
fin, Nora Roberts, William Gibson, Robin Cook,
Brian Jacques, Catherine Coulter, Stephen King,
Jacquelyn Mitchard, and many more!

Penguin Putnam Online is located at
http://www.penguinputnam.com

# PENGUIN PUTNAM
# NEWS

Every month you'll get an inside look at our
upcoming books and new features on our
site. This is an ongoing effort to provide you
with the most interesting and up-to-date
information about our books and authors.

Subscribe to Penguin Putnam News at
http://www.penguinputnam.com/ClubPPI